Best
Restaurants
Chicago

BY SHERMAN KAPLAN

Illustrations: Roy Killeen
Design: Lynne Parode

101 PRODUCTIONS
SAN FRANCISCO

Distributed to the book trade in the United States
by Charles Scribner's Sons, New York.

Published by 101 Productions
834 Mission Street, San Francisco, California 94103

Library of Congress Catalog Number 77-4978
SBN 0-89286-119-3

Restaurants
Alphabetical Listing

The Abacus, Chinese (Mandarin), $$, 10-11
The Atlantic, British Isles, $$, 12-13
The Bagel, Jewish, $, 14
The Bakery, Continental, $$$, 15
Barney's Market Club, American, $$, 16-17
Bengal Lancers, Indian, $$, 18-19
The Berghoff, German, $, 22
Blackhawk, American, $$, 20-21
Bon Ton Restaurant, Hungarian, $, 22-23
Bowl and Roll, American, $, 23
Cafe de Paris, French, $$, 24-25
The Cajun House, Cajun/Creole, $$, 26-27
Captain Nemo's, Sandwiches, $, 28
Casbah, Armenian, $$, 30-31
Chef Alberto's, Continental, $$, 32-33
Chez Paul, French, $$$, 34-35
Chicago Pizza & Oven Grinder Co., Italian/American, $, 29
The Cottage (Calumet City), Continental, $$$, 36
Cricket's, French/American, $$$, 38-39
Dai-Ichi, Japanese, $$, 40-41
Dianna's Oppa, Greek, $, 42
Don's Fishmarket (Skokie), Seafood, $$, 44-45
Doro's, Northern Italian, $$$, 46-47
Dragon Inn North (Glenview), Chinese (Mandarin), $$, 48-49
Eli's The Place for Steak, American, $$, 50-51
Eugene's, American, $$, 52-53
Fanny's (Evanston), Italian, $$, 54-55
Farmer's Daughter (Orland Park), Continental, $$, 56-57
Fond de la Tour (Oak Brook), French, $$$, 58-59
Four Torches, American, $$, 60-61
French Port, Seafood, $$, 62-63
Garden of Happiness, Korean, $$, 64-65
Gaylord India Restaurant, Indian, $$, 66-67
Gene & Georgetti, Steaks/Italian, $$ 68-69

Genessee Depot, American, $, 70
Giannotti's (Forest Park), Italian, $$, 72-73
Gino's East, Italian, $, 71
Grandma's Receipts, American, $$, 74
Great Gritzbe's, American/International, $$, 75
Greek Islands, Greek, $$, 76-77
Half Shell, Seafood, $, 80
Hana East, Japanese, $$, 78-79
Hobson's Oyster Bar, Seafood, $, 81
House of Bertini, Steaks, $$, 82-83
House of Hunan, Chinese (Mandarin/Hunan), $$, 84-85
Hungarian Restaurant, Hungarian, $, 86
The Indian Trail (Winnetka), American, $, 87
James Tavern (Northbrook), Early American, $$, 88-89
Jovan, French, $$$, 91
Kamehachi, Japanese, $$, 92-93
Khyber, Indian, $$, 94-95
La Bouillabaisse, French, $$, 96-97
La Cheminée, French, $$$, 98-99
La Choza, Mexican, $, 100
La Fontaine, French, $$$, 102-103
La Fontanella, Northern Italian, $$, 104-105
La Llama, Peruvian, $$$, 106
La Poêle d'Or (Arlington Hts.), Omelettes/Crêpes, $, 101
Lawrence of Oregano, Italian, $$, 108
Lawry's, American (Prime Rib), $$, 109
Le Bastille, French, $$$, 110-111
Lee's Canton Cafe, Chinese (Cantonese), $$, 112-113
Le Festival, French, $$$, 114-115
Le Français (Wheeling), French, $$$, 116-117
Le Perroquet, French, $$$, 118-119
L'Épuisette, French, $$, 120-121
L'Escargot, French, $$$, 122-123
Les Oeufs, Omelettes, $, 126
Le Titi de Paris (Palatine), French, $$$, 124-125
The Magic Pan, Crêpes, $, 127
Mategrano's, Italian, $$, 128-129
Mathon's (Waukegan), Seafood, $$, 130-131

Matsuya, Japanese, $, 132
Maxim's de Paris, French, $$$, 134-135
Miller's Pub, American, $$, 136-137
Mill Race Inn (Geneva), American, $$, 138
Miomir's, Serbian, $$, 139
Nantucket Cove, Seafood, $$, 140-141
New Japan, Japanese, $, 146
The Ninety-Fifth, French, $$$, 142-143
Northern China, Chinese (Mandarin), $$, 144-145
The Original Pancake House, Pancakes, $, 147
Ostioneria Playa Azul, Mexican, $, 149
The Palladion, Greek, $$, 150-151
The Ritz-Carleton, Continental/French, $$$, 152-153
R.J. Grunts, American, $, 154
Sage's East, Continental, $$, 156-157
Salzburger Hof, Austrian/Continental, $$, 158-159
Sauer's, German/American, $, 155
Sayat Nova, Armenian, $$, 160-161
The Silo (Lake Bluff), American, $, 162
Sparta Gyros, Greek, $, 163
Su Casa, Mexican, $$, 164-165
Sweetwater, French, $$$, 166-167
Taj Mahal, Indian, $$, 168-169
Tale of the Whale, Seafood, $$, 170-171
Tango, Continental/Seafood, $$$, 172-173
Tenkatsu, Japanese, $, 174
Thai Little Home Cafe, Thai, $$, 175
The Thai Restaurant, Thai, $$, 176-177
That Steak Joynt, Steaks, $$, 178-179
Toscano, Italian, $$, 180-181
The Tower Garden (Skokie), Continental, $$$, 182-183
Truffles, French, $$$, 184-185
Village Tavern (Long Grove), American, $$, 186-187
The Waterfront, Seafood, $$, 188-189
Wrigley Building Restaurant, Continental, $$, 190-191
Zlata's, Serbian, $$, 192-193
Zum Deutschen Eck, German, $$, 194-195
Zweig's (Des Plaines), Jewish, $$, 196-197

Introduction

It is not unusual for people to ask me, "What's a good restaurant for dinner tonight?" My answer is always the same: "What kind of food do you like, what are you in the mood for, and how much do you want to spend?" That is where this book will come in handy. You will find restaurants from storefront ethnic to continental elaborate, in all price ranges. The restaurants listed are in Chicago or its suburbs. Whether you are tourist, conventioneer or resident, *Best Restaurants of Chicago* will guide you to the right places.

Chicago has some fine restaurants. A few are without doubt among the best in the United States. But we are an inland city and while seafood restaurants abound, don't expect your red snapper to be fresh from dockside. All seafood served here, except perhaps for that pulled from Lake Michigan or other nearby waters, comes to the city on ice. It may not be frozen rock hard, but it will have been iced for a day or two before it is served to you with a sprig of parsley and a boiled potato. The exceptions to this rule, of course, are those restaurants which have live lobster and/or trout in tanks on the premises.

On the other hand, you have a right to expect the finest meat that the Midwest can provide. While the Chicago Stockyards are now only a vacant lot (the industry for its own good reasons, no doubt, has moved to Joliet, about 50 miles away), we get some of the best corn-fed beef you can find. Veal is expensive but fork tender. Poultry and pork in the right hands and the proper pot set taste buds tingling.

Our produce is, of course, seasonal. Hothouse tomatoes in the winter leave a pall on the palate of critical diners. Yet lettuce, spinach, cauliflower and a host of other vegetables are available fresh all year round thanks to a thriving produce industry here.

In short, Chicago is no better nor worse than scores of other cities when it comes to a supply of fresh foodstuffs. What sets us apart on our "broad shoulders" is the restaurant talent that abounds here. This guide reflects some of the best there is.

Although I make few specific comments about dress in the pages that follow, a good rule is to show the same respect to a restaurant which it shows to you. Generally, the more formal the menu and setting, the less casual should be the attire. Open shirt and jeans may be fine for a burger and fries, but not for veal Oscar. Where reservations are suggested, you might ask about a dress code rather than face any discomfort when you arrive.

As has been my custom in reviewing restaurants for WBBM Newsradio 78, all the restaurants in this book were first visited anonymously. I only identified myself after the check was paid so I could tour the kitchen and judge its cleanliness and the overall quality of the operation.

Most restaurants listed are also shown with their menus. While these prices were current at the time of compilation, in a business as financially volatile as food preparation, stated prices cannot be guaranteed.

Although this book represents the singular opinions of its author, there are many people to thank. A large debt is owed to my editor, Lynne Parode, for her help and patience. And this book could probably not have been written without the support of dinner companions who willingly allowed me to taste from their selections, of CBS management who gave me the go-ahead for broadcast restaurant reviews more than six years ago, and of course, the support of my wife Eileen, who has shared not only my dinners, but my life.

Sherman Kaplan

RATING SYMBOLS

To help you find a restaurant to match your budget for the evening, the selections are divided into categories of inexpensive, moderate and expensive, using the symbols shown below. The ratings are based on the price of an average meal in that restaurant, food only; cocktails, wine and tips would be extra. Unless the establishment is specifically a lunch spot, ratings reflect the average dinner cost. Prices quoted in this book were in effect at the time of publication and are subject to change at any time.

$ **UNDER $5** The food will be good as well as economical, but atmosphere and smooth service may be lacking at some of these restaurants.

$$ **UNDER $10** In this price range of $5 to $10, we expect some charm and atmosphere in addition to excellent food.

$$$ **OVER $10** At this price, we expect excellence in food, service and surroundings. Flaws should be minor.

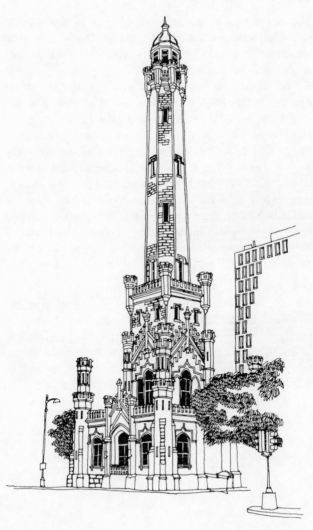

Water Tower

Chicago
THE ABACUS
Chinese (Mandarin) $$

This is the kind of place to visit with six or eight people. One good way is to call ahead, indicate what you want to spend and let owner Phil Shen plan your dinner. Or you can go through the menu yourself, choosing a fish course here, a fowl course there. Among favorites, I like the whole steamed fish in black bean sauce. The duck dishes, as you would suspect of a restaurant with Mandarin cuisine, are exceptional. The Abacus menu wisely indicates the authenticity of its dishes by using a rating system (five stars is the most authentic). The menu includes dozens of dishes representing the four great Chinese cuisines: Cantonese, Northern (Peking), Shanghai and Szechwan/Hunan. The Abacus is particularly well suited to beginners in the art of Chinese dining, but will also appeal to the sensibilities and taste of more experienced diners. An interesting wine list complements the menu.

THE ABACUS, 2619 North Clark Street, Chicago. Telephone: 248-6700. Lunch: 11:30 am-2:30 pm, Monday-Saturday. Dinner: 5 pm-11 pm, Monday-Thursday; until midnight Friday and Saturday; 1 pm-11 pm, Sunday. Cards: AE, BA, MC. Reservations recommended (some dishes require at least a day's notice). Free parking at nearby garage south on Clark Street. Full bar service.

201 *	Beef with Snow Peapods	C 5.25
202 ***	Mongolian Beef with Green Onions & Crispy Bean Threads	M 5.75
203 *	Tomato Pepper Steak in Black Bean Sauce	C 5.25
204 ****	Mandarin Hot Green Pepper Beef	M 5.25
205 ****	Szechwan Hot Diced Beef with Peanuts	Z 5.25
206 ***	The Abacus Steak on Sauteed Vegetables - A House Special	C 7.50
207 **	Beef with Fresh Spinach and Foo Yee	S 5.25
208 ****	Beef with Tofu and Chinese Mushrooms in Oyster Sauce	S 5.25
209 ****	Beef Mandarin with Assorted Vegetables	M 5.75
210 ****	Hunan Beef with Tea Sauce on Watercress	Z 5.75
211 *****	Chun King Spicy Beef with Wood Ears & Hot Pepper Sauce	Z 5.25

Fowl

301 *	Chicken with Snow Peapods	C 4.75
302 ****	Chan Pow Mandarin Chicken Ding with Cashews	M 4.75
303 ****	Szechwan Hot Diced Chicken with Peanuts	Z 4.75
304 ****	Mandarin Chow San See with Shredded Chicken, Bamboo Shoots and Chinese Mushrooms	M 4.75
305 ****	Cantonese Lemon Chicken	C 5.95
306 ****	Chicken Cantonese with Assorted Vegetables	C 5.95
307 *****	Chinese Fried Squab with Special Roasted Salt	S 7.95
308 ****	Crispy Home Style Smoked Tea Duck with Hoisin Sauce	Z 6.95
309 *****	Peking Duck (with Peking Duck Soup, 1.25 Per Person Extra)	M 18.00
310 *****	West Lake Duck - Love of the Oriental Gourmet	C 18.00
311 *****	Empress Dowager's Beggar's Chicken in Lotus Leaves and Baked in Clay (advance notice please)	M 25.00

Seafood

401 *	Shrimp with Lobster Sauce	C 6.25
402 **	Shrimp with Green Peas Mandarin	M 5.95
403 ****	Shrimp Mandarin with Assorted Vegetables	M 5.95
404 *	Sweet Sour Shrimp	C 5.95
405 ***	Mandarin Sizzling Rice Shrimp	M 5.95
406 *****	Szechwan Barbecued Shrimp in the Shell	Z 6.25
407 *****	Hunan Shrimp in Spicy Sauce	Z 6.25
408 *	Butterfly Shrimp	C 6.25
409 ****	Shrimp with Tofu and Chinese Mushrooms	M 5.95
410 *	Shrimp with Snow Peapods	C 5.95
411 **	Braised Shrimp with Chinese Vegetables	C 5.95
412 ****	Fresh Shrimp & Bean Thread Tango	C 5.95
413 ***	Scrambled Eggs with Shrimp and Oyster Sauce	C 5.95
414 ****	Sliced Fresh Conch Saute (advance notice please)	C Seasonal
415 *****	Braised Whole Fish with Chinese Greens	C Seasonal
416 *****	Braised Whole Fish with Hot Szechwan Sauce	Z Seasonal
417 ****	Shanghai Style Braised Whole Fish with Tofu	S Seasonal
418 *****	Sweet Sour Whole Fish	C Seasonal
419 *****	The Abacus Steamed Whole Fish with Black Bean Sauce	C Seasonal
420 **	Live Lobster Shanghai in Wine Sauce	S Seasonal
421 **	Live Lobster Cantonese	C Seasonal
422 *****	Hunan Spicy Lobster	Z Seasonal
423 ***	Crab Chinese Style	C Seasonal
424 ****	Clams Saute	S Seasonal
425 *****	Snails Saute	C Seasonal
426 ***	Abalone with Chinese Vegetables	M 6.95
427 ****	Cuttlefish with Chinese Greens (advance notice please)	C Seasonal
428 ***	Shanghai Stewed Turtle with Chicken and Ginger (advance notice please)	S Seasonal

Chicago
THE ATLANTIC
British Isles   **$$**

The British Isles do not have it so good anywhere else in the Chicago area. The Atlantic goes well beyond fish and chips in offering foods typical of England, Scotland, Wales and Ireland. Among the more tasty specialties are a giant helping of beef stew, authentic steak and kidney pie from England, and even fish and chips, although they aren't wrapped in a section of *The London Times*. Choose from a good selection of English and Irish beers and ales. The Atlantic also does a good job with traditional entertainment. A special menu for late snacks is offered after 10:30 pm. They even put together an Irish breakfast on Sunday mornings.

THE ATLANTIC RESTAURANT & PUB, 7115 West Grand Avenue, Chicago. Telephone: 622-3259. Hours: 4 pm-midnight, Monday and Tuesday; until 2 am Wednesday-Friday; 3 pm-2 am, Saturday; 11 am-1:30 am, Sunday. No cards. Reservations accepted. Street parking fairly convenient. Full bar service.

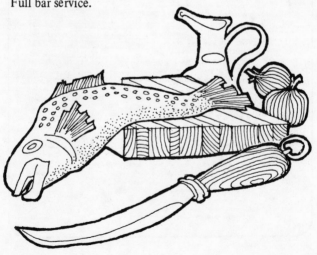

Wales

SHIP AND WALES **8.95**
A delicious combination of filet mignon and lobster tail evenly blended for the exceptional appetite. Soup, salad and dessert.

PRINCE OF WALES PLATTER **6.50**
Lean meaty baby back ribs cooked to perfection served in our Special Bar-B-Que sauce, with baked potatoe, salad, soup, dessert.

LADY GWEN, DELUXE **6.25**
A steer tenderloin filet mignon specially selected for the ladies, with flavor and tenderness. Served with soup, salad and dessert.

TOM JONES SPECIAL **9.50**
Wiggly lobster with meat of the genuine cold water tails. Delicate elegance. Includes homemade soup, salad and a dessert.

CARDIFF SUPPER **3.25**
Homemade Welsh beef stew, with chips.

WELSHMAN'S PARADISE **3.50**
Meat and potatoe pie with peas and chips.

ATLANTIC SHRIMPS "AHOY" .. **3.95**
Jumbo shrimp deep-fried in our special batter and served with chips.

England

THE ROYAL ATLANTIC **6.95**
An Imperial porterhouse steak of majestic flavor. Served with soup, fresh salad, baked potatoe, vegetable and dessert.

THE GUV **7.25**
A noble size of prime rib of beef, cooked in its natural juices with baked potatoe, vegetable, soup and salad. Dessert.

ENGLISH GRILL **6.50**
Thick lamb chop with bacon, sausage, black pudding, tomato, mushrooms, chips and our homemade soup. Chilled salad and a tempting dessert too.

THE DUCHESS **6.50**
A respected platter of Dover Sole served with our cream sauce of herbs and lemon. Baked potatoe. Carrots. Salad and dessert.

NUMBER "10" DOWNING STREET . **5.50**
Roast beef with Yorkshire pudding, boiled potatoe, vegetable, soup, salad and dessert.

PRIME MINISTER'S LUNCH **4.25**
Steak and kidney pie with chips and peas. En casserole.

LONDON'S BIG BEN **3.75**
Sheperd's pie. Chopped steak, onions, creamed potatoe with cheese. Served en casserole.

DARTMOUTH DINNER **3.25**
Cornish meat with vegetable, onion pastie, chips and peas.

HER MAJESTY'S DELIGHT **2.75**
British fish and chips, with peas.

Scotland

THE PIPERS LAMENT **5.25**
Two thick juicy pork chops charcoal broiled, served with roasted potatoes, green beans, and salad.

JOHN O'GROAT'S SPECIAL **4.95**
Short ribs of beef featuring a generous cut of select steer meat smothered in mushroom gravy. Served with soup, chilled salad and a delicious dessert.

FROM THE SCOTTISH COAST **4.95**
Baked haddock in butter with potatoes, carrots, homemade soup, salad and dessert.

SQUIRE McGREGOR'S BRUNCH .. **3.50**
Honey dipped chicken deep fried to a golden perfection and served in a basket with chips.

THE HIGHLANDER SPECIAL **3.25**
Black pudding deep-fried in our special batter. Peas and chips.

GLASGOW TREAT **2.95**
Scotch pie with peas and chips.

ABERDEEN BRUNCH **2.95**
Flaky pastie meat roll with onions, chips and peas.

Ireland

BUNRATTY TRADITIONAL FAVORITE **5.50**
Two tender young Spring Lamb chops served with a cup of homemade soup du jour, boiled potatoe, vegetable, salad and dessert.

WHERE THE SHANNON RIVER FLOWS **5.50**
Select red salmon steaks, in butter, with homemade soup, potatoe, carrots, salad and dessert.

PADDY'S DELIGHT **6.50**
Broiled Prime Sirloin Steak topped with mushroom caps and served with a cup of soup du jour, baked potatoe, vegetable, salad and dessert.

DUBLIN GRILL **3.95**
Irish bacon, sausages, black pudding, egg and chips.

IRISH SUPPER **3.50**
Pot pie of tender beef with vegetables, chips and Irish soda bread, served en casserole.

COUNTY MAYO SPECIAL **4.50**
A house specialty of liver and onions pan fried to tenderness, with boiled potatoe, salad.

IRISH SPECIAL **3.95**
Corned beef and cabbage with boiled potatoe, salad, Irish soda bread.

Served with dinners.
Complimentary relish tray, Irish soda bread,
bread and butter, bread rolls.

Chicago
THE BAGEL
Jewish

$

Home-style Jewish cooking is the watchword here. The few booths and counter stools are usually jammed with hungry people looking for good hearty fare at little cost. The most expensive dinner is no more than $5 and all dinners come with a basket of egg challa bread, soup or appetizer, salad, potato or vegetable, a beverage and dessert. The menu changes daily; regular selections include several kinds of fish, veal, chicken, duck, capon, tongue, meat loaf and short ribs. Some red horseradish on whitefish stuffed with gefilte fish will really clear the sinus cavities. The chopped chicken livers would be better with more schmaltz (chicken fat). On the plus side, good raisin custard is a dessert specialty. For smaller appetites there are individual servings of cheese or meat blintzes as well as several sandwiches. You should eat and be well at The Bagel; it's good for you.

THE BAGEL, 4806 North Kedzie Street, Chicago. Telephone: 463-7141. Hours: 5:30 am-9 pm, Monday-Saturday; 5:30 am-2 pm, Sunday. No cards. Reservations? You gotta be kidding. Street parking at meters is often tight. No alcoholic beverages.

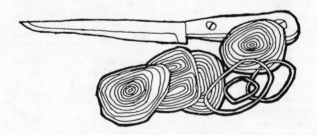

Chicago
THE BAKERY
Continental

$$$

If The Bakery is nothing else, it is consistent. Every time I visit I know that while cuisine will never rise above a certain level, it will never fall below a certain standard. The Bakery is the same today as it was the day it opened in 1963, although now the five-course dinner will cost $13. The Bakery's success stems from the hard work of chef Louis Szathmary, his brother Geza, their families and staff. Chef Louis is the more flamboyant, leaving everyday management to his brother, although he often tours the dining rooms in the evening chatting with dinner guests. There is no printed menu; while some items change daily, there are a number of constants. Waiters recite the evening's selections which include house pâté, soup, salad, main course with vegetables, dessert and coffee or tea. Most popular of the regular main courses are beef Wellington in a semisweet currant sauce, roast pork, and duck with cherry sauce. The steaming hot bouillabaisse is excellent when available. There is a modest but well thought out selection of wines or you may bring your own for a slight corkage charge.

THE BAKERY, 2218 North Lincoln Avenue, Chicago. Telephone: 472-6942. Hours: 5 pm-11 pm, Tuesday-Thursday; until midnight, Friday and Saturday; closed Sunday and Monday. No cards. Reservations required. Street parking. Wine only.

Chicago
BARNEY'S MARKET CLUB
American

$$

West of the Loop, Barney's has been host to convention-eers, politicians and other visiting firemen for decades. Even local Chicagoans are regularly drawn by Barney's good food and "Yes sir, Senator" atmosphere. Steaks and seafood predominate, led by a 24-ounce giant T-bone. Lobster usually weighs in at 2-1/2 pounds or more, with recent market prices in the $20 range. Expensive, certainly, but thought of by many as the best steamed lobster in the city. Dinners include appetizer, salad, baked or delicious shoestring potatoes, soup, rolls and relish assortment. Barney's Market Club is one of the few places left where you can get a real feel of Chicago's brawniness.

BARNEY'S MARKET CLUB, 741 West Randolph, Chicago. Telephone: 263-9795 and 263-9800. Hours: 11 am-midnight, Monday-Saturday; 4 pm-midnight, Sunday. Cards: AE, DC. Reservations recommended. Free doorman parking. Full bar service.

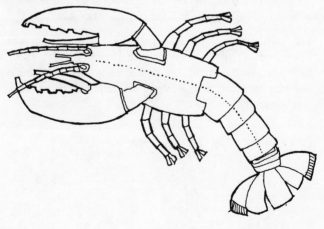

ROAST PRIME RIBS OF BEEF
From the Corn States Finest Prime Steers,
Mellow Aged.   Rich Tender Quality,   9.25

EXTRA HEAVY CUT PRIME RIB
OF BEEF AU JUS 13.00
Your Choice from the Well Done Outer Cut
to Red Rare Center Cut,

BIG
T-BONE
STEAK
24 OZ.
PRIME GRADED   11.95
A Regal Cut
that will Placate
the Most Eager
Appetite.

BEEF STROGANOFF
Tenderloin simmered in Burgundy Sauce,
topped with Sour Cream 8.25

SPECIAL CHOPPED PRIME BEEF STEAK
Served with Mushroom Sauce — made with
Madeira Wine 6.45

BROILED LAMB CHOPS
3 Thick Cut, Blue Ribbon Quality. Luscious   9.95

SEA & SHORE COMBINATION
8 oz. Top Butt Steak and 8 oz. King Crab
Legs from Alaska, Melted Butter 8.25

PEPPER STEAK A LA BARNEY'S
Slices of Prime Beef Tenderloin Sauteed in Butter
and simmered in a rich Madeira Wine Sauce.
Green Peppers and Mushrooms 7.95

BROILED PORK CHOPS ON TOAST (2 Chops)
Apple Sauce 7.95

BROILED PRIME TOP BUTT STEAK
¾ lb. Finest Quality, Aged to Perfection,
Broiled to Your Order 7.95

BARNEY'S PRIME SPECIAL SIRLOIN STEAK
Gourmet Cut, Well Over Full Pound, Our Special   9.75

PRIME SPECIAL SIRLOIN STEAK (Double Cut)
A Gastronomical Treat Particularly Favored   17.50

PRIME FILET MIGNON
Mushroom Caps and Onion Rings   9.75

BARBECUED SPARE RIBS
From Young Tender Pork Loins
Served with Our Special Tangy Sauce 7.95

Chicago
BENGAL LANCERS
Indian

$$

Visualize one of those old etchings showing the interior of a British officers' mess in colonial India and you will have a pretty fair idea of the Bengal Lancers. The first important Indian restaurant in Chicago, it has continued to draw a regular crowd over the years. The atmosphere is as cozy as can be. Delicious appetizers are an important part of the evening's dining. Samosa and pakora are exceptional; Bengal Lancers also serves one of the best chutneys around. For your main course selection, go with your inclination and you won't miss the mark. Curries can be prepared as mild or as hot as you like. If you take cocktails, the Pimm's Cup is prepared with particular attention; also featured are imported beers and ales.

BENGAL LANCERS, 2324 North Clark Street, Chicago. Telephone: 929-0500. Hours: 5:30 pm-10:30 pm, Tuesday-Thursday and Sunday; until midnight Friday and Saturday; closed Monday. Cards: AE, CB, DC, MC. Reservations suggested, particularly on weekends. Some street parking; garage at 2430 N. Clark (at discount). Full bar service.

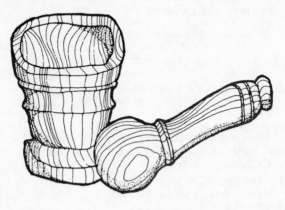

entrees

✳ all entrees will be accompanied by saffron rice with almonds, sombar, a vegetable and split pea side course ~ raitha, dahi (yoghurt) with a touch of fruit or vegetable ~ puris, a deep-fried puffed bread.

colonel skinner's chicken curry   5.50
a mildly spiced chicken curry cooked in butter, fresh tomato sauce and mogalai herbs. a dish worthy of bearing the name of the founder of the first bengal lancers.

probyn's beef curry   6.00
a medium spiced curry of tender beef in a tantalizing sauce named for the valiant deighton probyn, commander of the 11th lancers (probyn's horse) and winner of the victoria cross, the british commonwealth's highest honor.

kheema srinagar   5.50
medium spiced fine minced meat in a tasty combination of peas, tomatoes, other vegetables and spices named after the capital city of kashmir.

mysore lamb curry   6.00
a medium spiced curry. one of india's traditional currys made as only the bengal lancers can make it. named after the maharajah of mysore and the mysore lancers, headquartered in that city.

shrimp curry mountbatten   6.50
a spicey seafood curry of delicious shrimp, named after one of england's greatest sea lords, lord louis mountbatten, earl mountbatten of burma, admiral of the fleet, india's last viceroy and first governor-general of dominion of india.

vegetarian madras   5.00
it's easy to be a vegetarian in india for vegetables are plentyful and delicious throughout the year. the regiment's special subzi is medium spiced, combining a fabulous mixture of vegetables with exotic spices.

bhoona gohst   8.00
prime cut of beef, baked in special bengal lancers sauce over a dozen spices and herbs. north indian traditional cuisine yours for the asking.

malai jhinga   6.50
mildly spiced prawns cooked in coconut cream. popular from goa to cape camarin.

delhi lamb kabab   6.50
medium spiced, very tender and lean lamb cubes broiled to perfection over ten spices make this entree fit for the most discriminating palate.

tandoori chicken   6.85
medium spiced broiled chicken, absolutely the last word in cookery. a fantastic experience!

Chicago
BLACKHAWK
American

$$

Don Roth's Blackhawk is one of the few consistently good places in the Loop. It may be living off its past in some respects, but it is still part of the Chicago experience and well worth an evening's dining. There is an almost clockwork precision about some aspects of the Blackhawk. Not a place to dawdle, it's a good pre-theater spot for dinner and always attracts sports fans during Bulls and Blackhawks season. Beef is the byword here, especially the perfect filet mignon. The spinning salad bowl is a tradition, and no matter how many times you have seen the performance and heard the speech that goes with its preparation, it's fun to hear it one more time.

Close to shopping and theater on North Michigan Avenue, Don Roth's Blackhawk on Pearson brings the famous Blackhawk dining to the Near North Side. The only difference is that the Pearson restaurant has a salad bar instead of the spinning salad bowl.

DON ROTH'S BLACKHAWK, 139 North Wabash, Chicago. Telephone: 726-0100. Hours: 11 am-10:30, Monday-Saturday; 3:30-10:30, Sunday. Cards: AE, BA, CB, DC, MC. Reservations recommended. Parking at a nearby garage ($1 for all evening). Full bar service; good wine list.

DON ROTH'S BLACKHAWK, 110 East Pearson, Chicago. Telephone: 943-3300. Lunch: 11:30-2:30 pm, Monday-Saturday. Dinner: 5 pm-10:30 pm, Monday-Thursday; until 11 pm Friday; until midnight Saturday; 5 pm-9:30 pm, Sunday. Cards: AE, BA, CB, DC, MC; house accounts. Reservations recommended. Self-park garage west of restaurant ($1.25 after 5 pm). Full bar service.

from the open hearth broiler

u.s. prime sirloin steak (12 oz.) —
the king of them all — thick, juicy, tender, closely trimmed **9.95**

u.s. prime filet mignon (9 oz.) —
with fresh mushroom — everybody's favorite **8.75**

chopped steak from prime beef (10 oz.) —
topped with fresh mushroom **5.75**

"cold water" lobster tails
the tender, succulent "hard to get" kind with
freshly melted butter **10.50**

chicken breast teriyaki
with pineapple — polynesia at its best **5.75**

for those who want the best of both worlds

lobster & filet mignon **9.95**

boston schrod & filet mignon **8.25**

lobster & boston schrod **8.75**

BEEF OSKAR — a tantalizing taste treat: filet mignon, crabmeat,
asparagus, and our own bernaise sauce.
8.95

served with all entrees . . .

baked idaho potato —
seasoned with sour cream   **or**   the blackhawk's famous
and chives   **creamed fresh spinach**

or golden french fried potatoes

Chicago
THE BERGHOFF
German

$

This restaurant goes back almost 80 years. It is still serving some of the best sauerbraten, potato pancakes, sausages, stews, casseroles and chops you can find anywhere, much less in the heart of the Loop. Although the menu changes daily, the above-named specialties are constants and priced under $5. Good fish and steaks at somewhat higher prices are another integral part of the menu. Some dinners include only vegetables, others will offer a small salad, too. Appetizers can be as exotic as French snails, although the more affordable Bismarck herring are more in keeping with the place. Waiters are of the old school: efficient service without familiarity until you become a regular. Berghoff-made draft beer, light or dark, is splendid. If old-time comic-strip character Jiggs were ever in Chicago, this is where he would hang out to escape Maggie.

THE BERGHOFF, 17 West Adams, Chicago. Telephone: 427-3170. Hours: 11:30 am-9:30 pm, Monday-Saturday; closed Sunday. No cards. No reservations. Evening parking at 17 East Adams garage (at discount). Full bar service.

Chicago
BON TON RESTAURANT
Hungarian

$

Dark red curtains cover the lower half of the front windows and protect Bon Ton diners from the outside world of State Street. Inside this charming spot, located just a block or two north of the noisy Rush Street strip of nightclubs and show lounges, you will find a slice of Middle Europe. With influences that reflect a Magyar heritage, Hungarian foods and shish kebob transform the Bon Ton into something more than just another coffee shop. Of the two shish kebob house specialties, the lamb is the one to try. Both come showered with a mixture of shredded fresh parsley and onions, a side of rice and a vegetable. You won't go wrong with any of the other Hungarian dinners which include soup, salad and vegetable. And don't miss the piroshkees, those luscious meat-filled turnovers that are hard to stop gobbling down. But do save some room for dessert. Pastries are as light and delicate as anything you can imagine. If you have a sweet tooth, this is the place to satisfy your craving. If you are watching calories, take a deep breath and forget your diet this once. Because Bon Ton is as much pastry shop as restaurant, all their baked goods are available for carry-out.

BON TON RESTAURANT AND PASTRY SHOP, 1153 North State Street, Chicago. Telephone: 943-0538. Hours: 11 am-9:20 pm, Monday-Thursday; until 10 pm Friday and Saturday; closed Sunday. No cards. No reservations. Street parking. No alcoholic beverages.

Chicago
BOWL AND ROLL
American $

As the name suggests, the specialty here is soup and sandwiches. But there's more to it than that. The soups are all homemade, enormous, and a meal in themselves. The old-fashioned beef is loaded with chunks of roasted meat and large cuts of vegetables in a hearty broth. The chicken with noodles is always a treat. Sandwiches are served on thick slices of crusty French bread. Chopped liver is my favorite. If you still have room, try the deep-dish apple pie à la mode for dessert.

BOWL AND ROLL, 1339 North Wells, Chicago. Telephone: 944-5361. Hours: 11:30 am-9 pm, Tuesday-Thursday; until 11 pm Friday and Saturday; noon-9 pm, Sunday; closed Monday. No cards. No reservations. Parking available in local lots at exorbitant cost, but while you are there, you may as well stroll through Old Town and see the sights. No alcoholic beverages.

Chicago
CAFE DE PARIS
French

$$

Tucked inside a Near North Side apartment-hotel, Cafe de Paris does a consistently good job with a fairly imaginative menu. A small restaurant, the Cafe has a cozy sophistication lacking in much larger establishments. The house specialty is duckling à la Belasco, a classic preparation of the bird with crackling, crisp skin and marvelous orange sauce. Other favorites worth more than passing attention are tournedos Rossini and turbot Veronique. Table d'hôte dinners are inclusive from appetizer to dessert; à la carte selections are also offered. Among the sweet conclusions to your dining, don't pass up the profiterole, ice cream in puff pastry drizzled with dark chocolate sauce.

CAFE DE PARIS, 1260 North Dearborn Parkway, Chicago. Telephone: 943-6080. Hours: 5 pm-11 pm, Monday-Saturday; 4 pm-11 pm, Sunday. Cards: AE, BA, CB, DC, MC. Reservations required. Parking in adjacent lot. Full bar service.

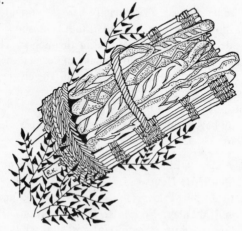

Table d'Hote Dinners

Appetizers

Filet of Herring in Fresh Sour Cream

Melon in Season   Consomme   Onion Soup

Chicken Liver Pate, Maison   Fresh Fruit Cup

Half Grapefruit   Boneless Sardines

Cream Vichyssoise .45   King Crabmeat Cocktail 1.35

Shrimp, Cafe or Red Sauce .85

Escargots Bourguignonne (6) 1.85

Shrimp Mignonette 1.25   Blue Points 1.50

Avocado with Shrimp 1.25   Avocado with Crabmeat 1.50

Le Caneton a La Belasco

DUCKLING A LA BELASCO 9.95

In all America, the Long Island Duck is the most esteemed, the "ne plus ultra" of succulence in duckdom. However, as a Historical note, these famous Ducks are not native to Long Island, but are descendants of the Imperial Chinese Ducks. These are Royal Ducks and as recently as 1873 their ancestors waddled about the Imperial Aviaries of China. A small lot of these ducks arrived in New York March 13, 1873 and thus the beginning of a Duck Dynasty in America. To this day the Long Island Duck Growers honor this date.

Roast Long Island Duckling has been a specialté of the Cafe De Paris over twenty-seven years, and every day many gourmets unknowingly honor this date, as well as please their palates, when they order Duckling a la Belasco.

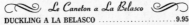

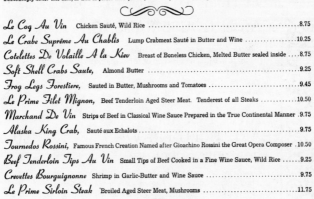

Le Coq Au Vin   Chicken Sauté, Wild Rice 8.75

Le Crabe Suprême Au Chablis   Lump Crabmeat Sauté in Butter and Wine 10.25

Cotelettes De Volaille A la Kiev   Breast of Boneless Chicken, Melted Butter sealed inside 8.75

Soft Shell Crabs Saute,   Almond Butter 9.25

Frog Legs Forestiere,   Sauted in Butter, Mushrooms and Tomatoes 9.45

Le Prime Filet Mignon,   Beef Tenderloin Aged Steer Meat. Tenderest of all Steaks 10.50

Marchand De Vin   Strips of Beef in Classical Wine Sauce Prepared in the True Continental Manner .9.75

Alaska King Crab,   Sauté aux Echalots 9.75

Tournedos Rossini,   Famous French Creation Named after Gioachino Rossini the Great Opera Composer .10.50

Beef Tenderloin Tips Au Vin   Small Tips of Beef Cooked in a Fine Wine Sauce, Wild Rice 9.25

Crevettes Bourguignonne   Shrimp in Garlic-Butter and Wine Sauce 9.75

Le Prime Sirloin Steak   Broiled Aged Steer Meat, Mushrooms 11.75

Caesar, Mixed Green, Steak Tomato, or Half Avocado Pear Salad
Garlic, Clear French or Thousand Island Dressing

Desserts et Cafe

French Pastries   Mocca Rum Layer Cake

Profiterolle   Creme de Menthe Parfait 1.35   Cherries Jubilee 2.25

Chocolate Sundae   Choice of Ice Cream   Snow Ball

Half Grapefruit   Brandy Ice 1.60   Fromage   Melon in Season   Mousse au Chocolat

Pot au Creme   Creme de Cocoa Parfait 1.35   Crepes Suzette 2.25

Chicago
THE CAJUN HOUSE
Cajun/Creole

$$

This is Chicago's only Cajun or Creole restaurant, but it is a representative adventure in Louisiana bayou cookery nonetheless. Dinners are served in a remodeled old home with an atmosphere something akin to a Tennessee Williams stage setting. The only thing missing is Spanish moss and tall swamp cyprus trees. The Cajun House has been serving peanut soup for a long time, well before President Carter made peanuts our national emblem. It is far superior to the rather ordinary Creole seafood gumbo. After salad, choose from the ten main-course selections. These include a seemingly out-of-place tournedos burgundy, which pays some tribute to the French antecedents of Louisiana cuisine.

CAJUN HOUSE SAUSAGE ... 9.25

Authentic Cajun sausage from Lafayette, La. Cajun House is proud to present a selection of three distinct types — all beef smoked . . . a fresh pork . . . and a white boudin (a mixture of pork and rice with Cajun seasoning). Served with white rice and the vegetable of the day.

CAJUN HOUSE BARBECUED PRAWNS 11.50
The House Specialty

The word barbecue is mis-leading — for in fact the shrimps are baked in almost every known spice and herb found in the kitchen. Pure vegetable oil, dry white wine, garlic and onion complete the array of ingredients — served with natural brown rice and grilled tomato.

CAJUN CATFISH with Hush Puppies............ 9.25

Catfish is truly favored by the Cajun appetite — caught in fresh water streams, breaded lightly and deep fried.

CHICKEN PONTALBA 9.25

Deboned chicken — pan fried and served on a bed of diced potatoes, ham, scallions and mushrooms with Bearnaise sauce. One of the most unique chicken dishes ever to be created!

Catfish is a house specialty, as are the barbecued prawns. But most interesting is chicken Pontalba, a classic New Orleans preparation. Among à la carte accompaniments, the hush puppies are great. If ice cream, pecans and Karo syrup are offered for dessert the evening you visit, snap it up.

THE CAJUN HOUSE, 3048 West Diversey Avenue, Chicago. Telephone: 772-1230. Hours: 5 pm-10:30 pm, Tuesday-Saturday. Closed Sunday and Monday. Cards: MC. Reservations required. Plentiful street parking nearby. Wine only; short but well-reasoned wine list is 100 percent domestic.

SHRIMP CREOLE............10.25

Fresh Gulf shrimp are simmered to perfection in a rich Creole sauce. Served with a bed of fluffy white rice.

CREOLE RED SNAPPER...... 9.25

Baked to perfection in lemon-butter, covered with Creole sauce and engulf by fluffy white rice.

BEEF TIPS CREOLE 9.50

Tips from the tenderloin are braised in a rich Creole sauce, encompassed by a ring of fluffy white rice. Fit for a meat eaters appetite.

CREOLE STUFFED EGGPLANT 9.95
(when available)

The eggplant is stuffed with a mixture of Titi shrimp, crab meat, onion, fine herbs, spices and bread crumbs— all of which is covered by a rich Creole sauce.

CHICKEN JAMBALAYA...... 8.75

A delightful dish featuring deboned chicken with a hint of shrimp, ham and dry white wine to enhance the flavor of the staple ingredients found in a Jambalaya — served En Casserole.

Chicago
CAPTAIN NEMO'S
Sandwiches $

This is the ultimate submarine sandwich shop. A large board behind the counter lists several sandwiches, most in the $2.25 to $2.50 range and all available in half-loaf form for about half the price. By the time you finish with a soft drink and some ice cream you would be hard-pressed to spend more than $3.50 a person. Sandwiches are built before your eyes on foot-long French loaves. They start with a dressing, your choice of a mild mustard or mayonnaise. Then come your selection of meats such as turkey, ham, bologna, hot meat loaf, plus cheeses, seasoned oil and vinegar dressing, onion, eggs, radishes, tomatoes, pickles, shredded lettuce ... a veritable garden of sandwich delights. If you really have an ambitious appetite, you can order the soup of the day for about half a buck. Often served is thick and steamy split pea in a broth that would make Julia Child take notice. What more can you say about a sandwich shop? A great deal in this case because there is a moral to be learned here. No matter what you do in life, do it well and your effort will be appreciated. I have never been in a restaurant where customers are greeted with such genuine friendliness and regard and where more pride is taken in what is being prepared. And yes, there is a real Captain Nemo who makes sure that all comers are well fed and satisfied.

CAPTAIN NEMO'S, 7367 North Clark Street, Chicago. Telephone: 973-0570. Hours: 11 am-9 pm, Monday-Saturday; closed Sunday. No cards. No reservations. Street parking. No alcoholic beverages.

Chicago
CHICAGO PIZZA AND
OVEN GRINDER COMPANY
Italian/American $

This is the only place I know of where pizza is served by the pound rather than by the diameter. The pizza is Chicago-style, deep dish with a puffy dough that rises up over the side of the baking pan. You get your pizza in either of two ways, sausage or vegetarian. The meat pizza is the better of the two, as the vegetarian can be a bit over-sauced with not enough cheese. On the plus side, the sauce is made fresh from tomatoes which have been crushed, simmered and spiced. Don't forget the grinders, which include an Italian combination and an incredibly gargantuan meatball sandwich loaded with garlic on a toasty long loaf. Man does not live by grinders and pizza alone, so splurge and get a salad. They are justly called "salad dinners" because one will feed a whole tableful of hungries. Mixed drinks, wines and beer are available. Finally, a bit of history. The Chicago Pizza and Oven Grinder Company is just across the street from a vacant lot on which once stood the garage made famous by the St. Valentine's Day Massacre.

CHICAGO PIZZA AND OVEN GRINDER COMPANY, 2121 North Clark Street, Chicago. Telephone: 248-2570 and 248-2672. Hours: 4 pm-midnight, Monday-Thursday; until 2 am Friday; noon-2 am, Saturday; 1 pm-midnight, Sunday. No cards; personal checks accepted with proper identification. Street parking difficult; garage nearby. Full bar service.

Chicago
CASBAH
Armenian

$$

The name and decor imply North African/Arabic culture, but the food, in fact, is Armenian. A small restaurant seating only about 70 people, Casbah is just a few doors from the heart of the busy New Town area which begins at the intersection of Clark, North Broadway and Diversey. What the menu does not explain, the service people most surely will. Among the excellent dinner choices, I particularly like the meat beorak, an Armenian version of lamb en croûte. There is really no way to go wrong here, because as exotic as the recipes and textures are, the ingredients are not that unfamiliar to Midwestern taste buds.

CASBAH, 514 West Diversey Parkway, Chicago. Telephone: 935-7570. Hours: 5 pm-11 pm, Sunday-Friday; until midnight Saturday. Cards: BA, CB, DC, MC. Reservations accepted. Two hours free parking at nearby Rienze Garage. Full bar service.

DINNERS

include:

HOMMOS OR DJADJIC
EGG-LEMON SOUP   TOSSED SALAD

ENTREES

SARMA   6.00
Grape leaves stuffed with rice and ground meat. Served
with yogurt.

KIBBEE   6.00
Cracked wheat blended with ground lamb, filled with
ground meat, onions and walnuts, and served with vegetables.

KIFTAH SHISH-KABAB   5.50
Marinated ground lamb and beef, broiled with tomato
and green pepper, served with pilaff.

KILIS KABAB   6.00
Marinated ground meat skewered alternately with eggplant, served with a special fresh tomato sauce and
rice pilaff.

MEAT BEORAK   6.50
Spiced meat, onions, tomatoes baked in a flaky dough.

ARMENIAN KABAB   7.20
Cubes of beef, green pepper, onions, eggplant and fresh
tomatoes baked without water. Served with rice pilaff.

BEEF OR LAMB SHISH-KABAB   7.00
Marinated cubes of lamb or beef, broiled with tomato,
green pepper, served with pilaff.

COMBINATION DINNER   6.50
Sarma, kibbee, and baked eggplant sauteed in olive oil,
onion, spices.

MAGLUBE — Weekends Only   6.00
Spiced rice cooked with cubes of lamb, cauliflower, and
pine nuts.

American or Turkish Coffee — Extra Turkish Coffee .45

Chicago
CHEF ALBERTO'S
Continental

$$

Chef Alberto is a hunter of some renown in Chicago and the walls of his beautiful restaurant boast some of the trophies he has taken. But don't expect braised lion or buffalo steak. Chef Alberto's specializes in excellent French and Italian cuisines. From among the dinner entrées, don't miss the duckling in orange sauce. The sauce carries a flavorful accent of Cognac that marries beautifully with the other ingredients. Veal Parmigiana is good, not exceptional. The veal picante is served in a rich lemon-butter sauce. Pepper steak is prepared with green peppercorns rather than sharply pungent black peppercorns. Pastas offer particular distinction. Canneloni Alfredo, stuffed with ground chicken and beef, is served in a creamy wine sauce garnished with sliced mushrooms. And don't miss the fettuccini Alfredo, which, as custom demands, is prepared tableside with fresh, sweet cream blended into the pasta. The wine list is small and not overpriced.

CHEF ALBERTO'S, 3200 North Lake Shore Drive in The Harbor House, Chicago. Telephone: 549-2515. Hours: 5 pm-midnight, Tuesday-Friday and Sunday; until 1 am Saturday; closed Monday. Cards: AE, DC. Reservations suggested weeknights, required on weekends. Parking in apartment-hotel garage (at discount). Full bar service.

Chef Alberto's Gourmet Dinners
ALL DINNERS INCLUDE APPETIZERS SOUP, SALAD AND PASTA

Melon and Prosciutto in Season   Chopped Chicken Livers Paté   Italian Antipasto
Tomato Juice   Iced Fresh Hawaiian Pineapple   Marinated Herring
Italian Minestrone Soup or French Onion Soup

Caesar Salad (Tossed at Table), Green Goddess or Chef's Salad Bowl

Fettuccini, Alfredo or Spaghettini, Bolognese with All Entrees

Coq Au Vin a la Bourguignonne, Wild Rice 7.75
Breast of Capon in Red Wine, Pearl Onions, Mushrooms, Wild Rice Dressing

Roast Long Island Duck, Flambeau (Half), Jus D'Orange . .   8.75
Wild Rice Dressing, Cognac Orange Sauce, Sweet Potato

Boneless Double Breast of Chicken a la Kiev (Our Own) . . .   7.75
Chicken a la Kiev, Handed Down from the Czar

Peppered Steak Burgundy 8.75
Filet Mignon Split, Fresh Green Peppers, Onions, Mushrooms, Tomatoes

Chicken Vesuvio (for garlic lovers) 7.25
Disjointed Chicken and Potatoes Sauteed in Olive Oil with Garlic, Dry Wine

Veal Cutlet a la Parmigiana 7.25
Cutlet Baked with Tomato Sauce, Mozzarella Cheese, Fried Egg Plant

Scallopine of Veal en Casserole 7.25
Fresh Mushrooms Sauce, Marsala Wine

Milk Fed Veal Medallions a la Picante 7.75
Seasoned Veal, Mushrooms, Lemon Butter Sauce

Chicken a la Cacciatore, Hunter Style 7.25
Disjointed Chicken, Onions, Mushrooms, Tomatoes, Italian Black Olives

Shrimp de Jonghe en Casserole 8.50
Sauteed in Dry Wine with Garlic Toasted Bread Crumbs

Fried Calamari (Squid), Butter and Lemon Sauce 7.95

Canneloni, Alfredo en Casserole Au Gratin 6.95
Crepes Stuffed with Chicken and Beef, Mornay Sauce

Manicotti, en Casserole Salsa Pomidori 6.95
Crepes Stuffed with Ricotta Cheese, Tomato Sauce

Chicago
CHEZ PAUL
French

$$$

The problem with old, established restaurants is that due to sheer longevity they run the risk of a "living on past reputation" accusation. This accusation is sometimes made of Chez Paul, which may be the oldest of the posh French restaurants in the city. In truth, Chez Paul has never impressed us with the level of culinary grandeur achieved by some other haute cuisine restaurants, and yet, whenever we have visited, our dinners have not been without their little pleasures. For one thing, the restaurant is beautiful, housed in an historic old Chicago town house. Service is precise without familiarity; many former Chez Paul waiters and captains have gone on to open their own fine establishments. Chez Paul presents one of the broadest menu selections of any French restaurant in the city. The à la carte menu lists house specialties in bold red color. Among appetizers, for instance, I like the seafood crêpe in a sublime cream sauce. Onion soup is baked in the crock with a thick cheese topping. For entrées, fish and veal are well handled; a daily unlisted special is also offered in addition to menu choices. Chez Paul has always been popular with the dining public at large, but seems to do exceptionally well in handling businesspeople who are looking for the perfect place to entertain clients.

CHEZ PAUL, 660 North Rush Street, Chicago. Telephone: 944-6680. Lunch: 11:30 am-2:30 pm, Monday-Friday. Dinner: 6 pm-10:30 pm, Monday-Friday; until 11:30 pm Saturday; until 10:30 pm Sunday. Cards: AE, BA, CB, DC, MC. Reservations required. Valet parking. Cocktail lounge open each evening until midnight; comprehensive wine list.

Les Hors d'Oeuvres

Froids : Stuffed Avocado Parisienne 3.50   Shrimp cocktail 3.25

Alaskan King Crabe Remoulade 3.75   Blupoints on Half Shell 2.50

Paté de Foie Gras Truffé 7.75   Terrine de Canard Truffée 2.50

Iranian Beluga Caviar 8.75   Heart of Palm Vinaigrette 2.50

Chauds : Baked Shrimps à la Papa Paul 3.50   Escargot Chablisienne 3.75

Quiche Lorraine 2.75 Crêpes aux Fruits de Mer Dieppoise 2.50

Baked Oysters Bercy 3.25   Baked Alaskan Crabe 3.75

Endives Flammandes 3.50

Les Potages

Potage du Jour 1.50   Soupe à l'oignon Gratinée 1.95

Bisque de Homard 2.25   Vichyssoin Glacée 1.75

Les Poissons et Crustacés

Turbot Sauté Armenonville 10.50   Dover Sole Meunière or Amandine 10.25

Homard Cardinal 10.75   Cuisses de Grenouilles Provençales 8.75

Filet de Sole Chez Paul 10.25   Turbot poché Hollandaise 10.50

Whitefish Amandine 7.25   Langoustines Grillées Nantua 9.75

Les Grillades

Filet de Bœuf Bordelaise or Béarnaise 10.50   Double Lamb Chops 11.50

Lamb Chops à la Papa Paul 11.50   Le Steak Minute Maitre d'Hotel 8.50

Chateaubriand Bouquetière 24.50   Le New York Sirloin 10.25

Les Entrées

Escallopes de Veau Normande 8.25   Filet au Poivre Flambé Annaguae 10.95

Roast Rack of Lamb (for two) 24.95   Canard rôti à l'orange 8.50

Filet de Bœuf à la Colbert 10.75   Foie de Veau Lyonnaise 7.25

Escallopes de Veau au citron 8.25   Tripes à la Mode de Caen 6.50

Ris de Veau Maréchal 8.75   Rognons de Veau sautés Napoléon 7.25

Les Salades

Cresson et Tomates 2.25   Endives Belges 2.00   Salade d'Epinard 2.00

Salade Jean Paul 2.75   Salade Ceasar 2.25   Salade d'Avocado 2.00

Roquefort or 1000 isles xtra .95

Calumet City
THE COTTAGE
Continental

$$$

Although Chicago's North Side and suburbs have more really good restaurants than the South Side, don't discount that section of metro Chicago for fine dining. Consider, for instance, The Cottage and its old country inn atmosphere. The authentic antiques and hand-finished furnishings gathered by proprietors Jerry and Carol Buster add to the appeal. Yet the food remains the standout. Although the menu may change from evening to evening, you should have no trouble picking something excellent from the half dozen or so entrées offered. I love the steak Madagascar, a pepper steak with mild green peppercorns rather than the harsher black. Mock lobster is really monkfish that will fool no one, but it still tastes good. The Cottage schnitzel is pork, not veal. Dinners begin with a beautiful appetizer, followed by fresh soup of the day and salad. They range from about $11 to $14; add $1.75 more if you want one of the luscious desserts. The Cottage is loaded with charm, but more than that, standards of food and service are kept high.

THE COTTAGE, 525 Torrence Avenue, Calumet City. Telephone: 891-3900. Hours: 5 pm-10 pm, Tuesday-Thursday; until 11 pm Saturday and Sunday; closed Monday. No cards. Reservations recommended. Free parking in adjacent lot. Full bar service; good wine list.

Wrigley Building

Chicago
CRICKET'S
French/American

$$$

To the diner expecting plush surroundings, thick-pile carpeting and dim romantic lighting, Cricket's will come as a surprise. The atmosphere is decidedly masculine, almost "clubby." The place reminds me of taverns that used to be called "tack rooms," with their horseracing memorabilia—except at Cricket's the memorabilia includes baseball, football, newspapers and even earth-moving toys suspended from beams or attached to walls. Food and service are exceptional. Waiters and captains seem to anticipate every need, from replenishing an exhausted supply of hot rolls to topping up a glass of wine. The à la carte menu includes some beautifully prepared selections. Braised sweetbreads are served in an elaborate financière sauce of wine, bacon and green olives. The English sole is perfectly complemented by a cream sauce with delicate white seedless grapes. Other sauces, such as bigarade or Madeira, stand up well with their respective meats—duckling for the orange-based bigarade and beef in pastry for the more pungent Madeira. Soups, such as the cold crème Senegalaise or the delicate consommé, are perfect preparations. Among appetizers, I like the seafood crêpe with just a hint of curry. Sometimes featured among daily selections is a hot chicken pâté which is coarsely ground and baked in pastry. Desserts, not listed on the menu, include crêpes suzette, fresh fruits in season and a creamy, sweet chocolate pudding. A good selection of wines complements the menu.

CRICKET'S, 100 East Chestnut (in the Tremont Hotel), Chicago. Telephone: 751-2400. Lunch: noon-2:30 pm, Monday-Saturday. Dinner: 6 pm-10:30 pm, Monday-Thursday; until 11:30 pm Friday and Saturday. Sunday brunch: 11 am-2:30 pm. Cards: AE, BA, CB, DC, MC. Reservations required. Valet parking ($3). Full bar service; good wine selection.

STEAKS AND CHOPS

Steak au Poivre, Vert	10.75
Filet Mignon	10.50
Burger au Cricket	7.00
Steak Diane	11.25
Minute Steak	9.75
Lamb Chops	12.50

FISH

English Sole Poché Veronique	10.25
Red Snapper Sauté, Fine Herbes	8.50
Whitefish Grillé, Choron	8.25
Brook Trout Sauté, Amandine	8.75

ROASTS

Rack of Lamb for Two, Bouquetiere	per person 14.50
Long Island Duckling, Bigarade	9.25
Filet of Beef au Croute, Sauce Madiére	10.75
Roast Chicken for Two	8.25
Baby Squab farci, aux Grapes	per person 11.75

SPECIALTIES

Tournedos, a la Cricket	10.50
Chicken Hash, Mornay with Wild Rice	7.50
Sweetbreads Braisé, Financiére	8.75
Escallopine of Veal, Charleroi	9.50
Calf's Brains Sauté, aux Capers	8.50
Lobster Tail, Sauce Americaine	12.50
Veal Chop, Mascotte	10.75

garniture of vegetables du jour served with main courses

Chicago
DAI-ICHI
Japanese

$$

Located near the Conrad Hilton Hotel, Dai-Ichi is a convenient spot for conventioneers looking for something different. At the same time it happens to be a fairly diversified Japanese restaurant that goes well beyond the routine hibachi steak house. True, you can sit at one of the hibachi tables and enjoy a satisfying dinner. Or you can roam through the fairly ambitious menu and try something more exotic. Tempura is always a good start for those unfamiliar with Japanese cuisine and a continuing favorite with those who are. Some say tempura cooking was introduced to Japan by early Portuguese traders; other food historians say the tradition of vegetables and shrimp deep-fried in batter goes back earlier in Japan's history. Whatever the case may

ALA CARTE DINNER
Includes – Salad, Rice & Tea

TROUT SHIOYAKI	Baked with a rock salt crust to enhance the delectable natural flavor.	2.95
SALMON "		3.00
SALMON TSUTSUMIYAKI (Broiled & wrapped in foil with tomato, spinach, onion & spices) You'll be back again!		4.00
CHICKEN TERIYAKI	Specially Marinated with Wine, Sweetened Soy Sauce, & spices. Sauteed & served with Oriental Vegetables.	2.85
PORK TENDERLOIN "		3.85
TROUT "		3.05
SALMON "		3.25
FILET MIGNON "		5.75
SIRLOIN "		5.50
LOBSTER "		7.00
LOBSTER TOKYO YAKI (Itomeyaki Lobster Broiled with Onion, Mushrooms, & Cheese) A winner!		7.50
SANMA SHIOYAKI (Pipe Mackerel baked)		3.60

be, properly prepared tempuras are a joy; at Dai-Ichi, you'll get a delicate, airy batter around crisp vegetables or tasty prawns. Among the beef dishes that I like is inakayki, steak marinated in a ginger-spiked soy sauce before broiling. The atmosphere at Dai-Ichi is always quite pleasant, whether you choose the teahouse setting or the hibachi tables.

DAI-ICHI, 512 South Wabash, Chicago. Telephone: 922-5527. Hours: 11:30 am-10:30 pm, Monday-Thursday; 11:30 am-11 pm Friday; 5 pm-11 pm, Saturday; 5 pm-9:30 pm, Sunday. Cards: AE, CB, DC, MC. Reservations suggested. Garage parking nearby. Full bar service; wine, sake and Japanese beer.

DINNER MENU

Includes: flaming Shrimp Oni-Gara-Yaki
soup, salad, Rice, Tea, & Dessert

AUTHENTIC SUKIYAKI DINNER 6.00
(Tender Cuts of Beef, Exotic Japanese Vegetables, Soybean Cake, Mushrooms, & Hakusai; All delicately Broiled in the special Sukiyaki Sauce).

TEMPURA DINNER 6.50
(Dipped in Batter, Delicately Cooked in a pure Sesame Oil at a high degree temperature creating the crispness of a light snowflake but Paradoxically Piping Hot, Melting in your mouth).

SASHIMI (IN SEASON) 5.50
(slices of Fresh Fish Served A La Natural)

TONKATSU (PORK TENDERLOIN in a light crispy bread coating). 6.25

INAKAYKI (SIRLOIN STEAK Marinated in a ginger sauce). 7.95

BEEF TERIYAKI (SIRLOIN STEAK with a Teriyaki sauce). 6.75

Chicago
DIANNA'S OPPA
Greek $

Petros Kogeonos is probably the most flamboyant character in Chicago's Halsted Street/South Greektown neighborhood. Everyone is "cousin" to Petros. But aside from the character of its proprietor, Dianna's Oppa creates one of the cheeriest settings in Chicago for good Greek food. The restaurant looks like a Greek town square brought indoors. Waiters bustle back and forth between tables and kitchen calling out "Oppa!" ("Olé!") with each flaming of the popular appetizer saganaki (kaseri cheese flamed with brandy). The best deal in the house is the combination platter for $3.95, or, go with several people and order family-style. For $6.25 per person you are served avgolemono soup, Greek salad with tomatoes, lettuce and feta cheese, saganaki, gyros, pastitsio, mousaka, dolmades, rice, vegetables, plus braised lamb or beef.

DIANNA'S OPPA, 212 South Halsted, Chicago. Telephone: 332-1225 or 332-1349. Hours: 11 am-2 am, daily. Cards: AE. Reservations accepted. Free parking lot across the street. Full bar service; Greek wines.

Marshall Field Clock

Skokie
DON'S FISHMARKET
Seafood

$$

Who would expect to find a really great seafood restaurant in a Howard Johnson's motel, much less in Skokie? Well, folks, that's what we've got. The decor is typical fish restaurant a la Chicago; a recreation of a New England fish shanty with the usual trappings of weathered board, nautical fittings, polished wood tables and captain's chairs. Yet the food at Don's is so good the decor could be steel mill coffee shop and it would still be sensational. The fish is as fresh as you can get and still be in the Midwest. Pick from a daily catch that often includes snapper, Boston sole, lemon sole, trout, salmon, lake perch, etc. Striped sea bass broiled over charcoal is a real winner. Soft-shelled crabs in butter and almonds practically scream out their succulence. Check the daily chalkboard listing to see what's what. Wonderfully crusty bread and New York bialys, topnotch salad with baby shrimp and crumbled bleu cheese dressing, plus incredibly caloric desserts complete a fine dinner menu.

DON'S FISHMARKET AND PROVISION COMPANY, 9335 Skokie Boulevard (in the Howard Johnson's Motor Hotel), Skokie. Telephone: 677-3424. Lunch: 11:30 am-2:30 pm, Monday-Friday. Dinner: 5 pm-11 pm, Monday-Thursday; until midnight Friday and Saturday; 4 pm-10:30 pm, Sunday. Cards: AE, BA, MC. Reservations required. Free parking lot. Full bar service; good wine list and house wines.

STEAKS & COMBOS

What all these Crabs, you're probably wondering what's our beef?

Filet Mignon, 9 oz. **7.50**
A concession to diehard beefeaters.

Scampi Combo **8.50**
Scampi and butt steak.

Schrod Combo **7.50**
Fresh Boston baby haddock and butt steak.

Crab Combo **7.95**
King crab legs and claws with butt steak.

SHELLFISH

A note from the Lobster "I can't stand these crabs. Get me out of here!"

Live Maine Lobster, 1¼ lbs. **69.42***
Specify broiled or boiled.
*(Unless you can negotiate a better deal with your waiter—they're push overs.)

Two Live Maine Lobsters **69.43***
One male, one female, or two we're not sure about.
*(or possibly less.)

Whole Dungeness Crab **7.95**
Named after our owner.

Prawns in a Pan **7.95**
We broil our tails for you.

Alaska King Crab Legs and Claws
One full lb. **7.95**
If you think Betty Grable's legs are great, wait 'til you see these.

Chicago
DORO'S
Northern Italian

$$$

Don't let the rich gaudiness of Doro's decor put you off. This is a magnificent restaurant with outstanding northern Italian cuisine. Subtleties lacking in interior decoration are not lacking in the food. Fresh pastas are made in one of the most elaborate and well-designed restaurant kitchens I have ever seen. Ravioli al burro e salvia (ravioli pillows in butter and sage sauce) are exquisitely delicate, among other delicious choices. Seafood is given special attention, from storage in specially designed coolers to individual preparation. The extensive menu also features a large selection of veal, chicken and beef dishes. Service can sometimes be irregular; we once had our pasta brought with the main course, not before. Yet attention to culinary detail otherwise marks Doro's as one of the best.

DORO'S, 871 North Rush Street, Chicago. Telephone: 266-1414. Lunch: noon-3 pm, Monday-Friday. Dinner: 6 pm-10:30 pm, Monday-Thursday; until 11 pm Friday and Saturday; closed Sunday. Cards: AE, BA, CB, DC. Reservations required. Valet parking. Full bar service.

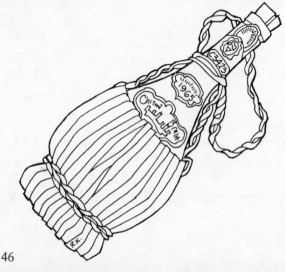

Vitello
VEAL

Piccata Lombarda — 7.50
Scaloppine Sauted With White Wine, Lemon And Butter.

Scaloppine Saute Florio — 8.00
Scaloppine Sauted With Mushrooms And Marsala.

Bracioline Di Vitello — 8.00
Veal Birds Stuffed With Cheese And Prosciutto.

Saltimbocca Alla Romana — 8.00
Scaloppine Sauted With Prosciutto, Sage And White Wine.

Fegato Alla Veneta — 7.50
Calf's Liver Sauted With Onions And White Wine.

Costoletta Di Vitello Alla Milanese — 8.00
Breaded Veal Chop Sauted.

Scaloppini Alla Sorrentina — 8.00
Scaloppine Sauted With Eggplant, Prosciutto And Cheese.

Costoletta Parmigiana — 8.50
Veal Chop With Tomato Sauce And Mozzerella Cheese.

Costoletta Al Madeira — 8.50
Veal Chops With Sauce Madeira.

Costoletta Valtostana — 9.00
Stuffed Veal Chop With Prosciutto And Cheese.

Animelle Saute — 9.00
Sweetbreads, Saute Meuniere.

Cervella Al Burro Nero — 8.25
Calf's Brains With Black Butter And Capers.

Manzo
BEEF

Medaglioni Di Bue Rossini — 11.50
Sauted Filet With Pate.

Medaglioni Choron — 11.50
Broiled Filet Mignon With Artichokes And Sauce Bernaise.

Steak Diane, A la Doro's — 10.25

Entrecote Nicoise — 11.50
New York Sirloin Sauted With Anchovies And Olives.

Entrecote All' Italiana — 11.00
New York Sirloin Sauted With Peppers, Mushrooms And Onions.

Steak Au Poivre Flambe. — 11.50

Pesce
FISH

Trancia Di Spigola Saute O Broiled — 7.00
Striped Bass Sauted Or Broiled.

Scampi Fra Diavolo — 8.25
Jumbo Shrimps In Spicy Red Sauce.

Pesce Del Lago Alla Griglia — 6.75
Broiled Lake Superior White Fish.

Sogliola Inglese Colbert — 8.50
Dover Sole Sauted In Butter, Maitre D'.

Zuppa Di Pesce — 8.50
Assorted Fish Casserole.

Trota Meuniere — 7.25
Fresh Rainbow Trout, Saute Meuniere.

Rane Provencale — 7.75
Frog Legs, Provencale.

Filetti Di Sogliola Bonne Femme — 8.25
Filets Of Gray Sole With Champagne Sauce And Mushrooms.

Lobster Tail — Priced According To Market
Broiled African Lobster Tail.

47

Glenview
DRAGON INN NORTH
Chinese (Mandarin) $$

The newest and best of a three-restaurant chain (Dragon Inn and Dragon Seed are the other two), Dragon Inn North offers consistently fine Mandarin, Hunan and Szechwan cuisine. It's true, I still disagree with the owners over preparation of the shrimp Hunan (too undercooked for my taste), but other than that I've never had a thing go wrong. There are more than 50 entrées on the comprehensive menu plus exotic appetizers and simmering soups. Let your waitress make suggestions if you are confused, or call at least a day ahead and ask for the marvelous Peking duck as a main course to build around. Another great choice is the smoked tea duck with crisp skin and dusky-flavored dark, rich meat. Incidentally, Dragon Inn is a worthy runner-up if you are on the Far South Side; Dragon Seed has a very good preparation mid-North.

DRAGON INN NORTH, 1650 Waukegan Road, Glenview. Telephone: 729-8383. Hours: 11:30 am-10 pm, Tuesday-Thursday; until midnight Friday; 6 pm-midnight, Saturday; noon-10 pm, Sunday; closed Monday. Cards: AE, CB, DC. Reservations suggested, especially on weekends. Free parking lot. Full bar service.

DRAGON INN, 18431 South Halsted, Glenwood. Telephone: 756-3344. Hours: same as for Dragon Inn North. Cards: AE. Reservations suggested. Free parking lot. Full bar service.

DRAGON SEED, 2300 North Lincoln Park West (in the Belden Stratford Hotel), Chicago. Telephone: 528-5542. Lunch: noon-2:30 pm, Tuesday-Friday. Dinner: 5 pm-11 pm, Tuesday-Thursday; until midnight Friday and Saturday; noon-10 pm, Sunday; closed Monday. No cards. Reservations accepted. Street parking; can be difficult. No alcoholic beverages; BYOB or from restaurant across lobby.

mandarin dishes

Chicken with Walnuts	$4.50
Chicken with Cashew Nuts	4.50
Chicken with Sizzling Golden Rice	4.50
Diced Chicken with Bean Sauce	4.50
Sliced Chicken with Black Mushrooms and Bamboo Shoots	4.95
Shredded Chicken with Bean Sprouts	3.95
Velvet Chicken	4.95
Peking Duck	18.00
Sliced Chicken with Pea Pods	4.50
Crispy Duck (half)	5.95
Shrimp Saute	6.95
Shrimp & Kidneys Saute	5.95
Shrimp with Peas	5.95
Shrimp with Sizzling Golden Rice	5.95
Sea Cucumber with Sizzling Golden Rice	5.95
Shrimp with Tomato Ginger Sauce	6.95
Sliced Fish Filet with Pea Pods	5.25
Crab Mandarin	5.95
Shredded Beef with Green Pepper	4.50
Filet Mandarin with Oyster Sauce	6.25
Lady's Portion	4.95

Chicago
ELI'S THE PLACE FOR STEAK
American

$$

Remember when you were little and your mother always said, "Eat your liver, it's good for you!"? If Mom had fixed liver like Eli's you would have gobbled it down and asked for seconds. At least one prominent restaurateur I know calls Eli Shulman "the restaurateur's restaurateur" primarily because of the calves liver. Eli's, as the name implies, is also a steak house (my favorite is the sirloin butt). Eli probably knows everybody in town; his restaurant and lounge has become a regular stop on the celebrity circuit. The food happens to be pretty good, if not all that exotic. So if you want a glimpse of Shecky, Buddy or Don when they are in Chicago, Eli's is the place for steaks and staring.

ELI'S THE PLACE FOR STEAK, 215 East Chicago, Chicago. Telephone: 642-1393. Lunch: 11:30 am-2:30 pm, Monday-Friday. Dinner: 4 pm-1 am, Sunday-Saturday; closed Monday. Cards: AE. Reservations required. Parking in building garage. Full bar service.

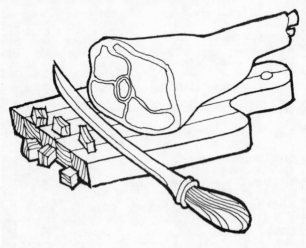

Entrees of the Open Hearth Broiler

Broiled Chopped Steak, Esther
Freshly Chopped Sirloin, Made from a Recipe
Handed Down Thru the Years That Brings Out That Old
World Flavor "A Must" 6.95

The Ladies Steak a la Mignon
For the More Petit Appetite, Prime Center Cut
Beef Tenderloin, Broiled to Her Taste 8.95

Old Fashioned Hamburger Patties a la Essie
Years Ago They Called Them Cutletten, Now the Same Old Flavor
with a New Name 6.95

Filet Mignon of Beef Tenderloin (Prime Center Cut)
A Borrowed French Idea, Magnificently Portrayed by
Prime Native Beef Tenderloin 9.95

Top of the Sirloin Butt Steak (Center Cut)
Open Hearth Broiled, Crisp Onion Rings 8.95

Broiled Jr. N. Y. Strip Sirloin Steak
Tender and Delicious 9.95

Broiled Fancy French Cut Double Lamb Chops
Extra Thick, Prime Loin Lamb Chops, Mint Jelly 9.25

Broiled New York Cut Strip Sirloin Steak   Mushroom Cap,
Our Finest Steak, This is Truly the King of all Steaks 10.95

Chateaubriand Le Bearnaise   (for two)
A Full Center Cut Tenderloin Filet That Truly Fits the Bill for any
Special Occasion 19.95
with Vegetable Bouquetiere 21.95

Entrees of Distinction

CALVES LIVER, ELI
Tops in Quality - Tops in Freshness - Tops in Taste
Sliced Calves Liver Sauteed with Onions, Green Peppers and
Mushrooms "Don't Hesitate" Delicious 7.95

BREADED VEAL CUTLET
Tender Veal, Breaded and Delicately Seasoned
Tomato Sauce, Candied Carrots 7.95

ELI'S SPECIAL SIRLOIN STEAK
Chared and Seasoned with Ground Pepper Corns
To Please the Spicy Taste Buds 10.95

Chicken Creole
Boneless Breast of Chicken, Topped with Creole Sauce 6.95

Roast Prime Native Rib Eye of Beef, Natural au Jus
A Thick Eye Cut of Corn Fed Prime Beef at its Finest 9.95
Junior Cut 7.95

Tournedos of Prime Beef Tenderloin   Brown Butter Saute,
A Feature of the House, Twin Center Cuts of Succulent Tenderloin 9.45

Bar - B - Que Genuine Canadian Baby Back Ribs
A Whole Slab of Tender Ribs, Smoked in the Old Fashioned Way 7.45

Italian Pepper Steak   Sauce au Vin Rouge, Sliced Tenderloin of Beef,
Mushrooms, Tomatoes and Green Peppers in Wine Sauce 9.45

Chicago
EUGENE'S
American

$$

If Damon Runyon had been in the restaurant racket, this would have been the kind of place he'd run. True, Eugene's is in a very posh neighborhood, but while there are some items for big-time spenders, there are moderate selections for less well-heeled guys and dolls. When you approach Eugene's do so with a sense of humor since that's what the boss did. Note references on the menu to Harry the Horse, Benny the Book, Big Julie, et al. If you want only a snack try Nathan Detroit's hamburger and a salad for $3.50 or chili Feets Kaplan for only 95 cents a bowl. Crêpes, steaks, chops and fish make up much of Eugene's menu, which covers most everything but stops short of a rap in the mouth and a knuckle sandwich. Before or after dinner there's always good entertainment in the lounge. Chances are you'll like Eugene's . . . or else, see!

EUGENE'S, 1255 North State Parkway, Chicago. Telephone: 944-1445. Hours: 5 pm-1 am, Monday-Thursday; until 2 am Saturday; until midnight Sunday. Cards: AE, BA, CB, DC, MC; house accounts. Reservations required. Valet parking. Full bar service.

Fishes and Shellfishes

EUGENE'S Most Magnificent Seafood Crepe 6.95
Red Snapper, Dijonaisse, is served in honor of Big Joe the Dealer 5.95
Frog Legs Provéncale, Given the Moniker by Morton the Masher 6.95
Dover Sole which is fixed with a special sauce of Shrimp and Mushrooms named Norman Across the Hall 8.50
Dover Sole saute with an unusual sauce of melted down butter 7.95
Broiled Alaskan King Crab Legs, with a butter sauce or perhaps it is your choice of a mustard sauce; the personal choice of Tommy the Gunsel 6.95
Soft Sell Sollie's Shrimp de Jonghe or John, if you are of the mind 6.50
Sam the Gonoph's Maine Lobster, boiled in beer or broiled (at prevailing prices)
Cold Maine Lobster, Finicky Phil's personal selection is served with Lobster Mayonnaise—at market

The Big Beef

Beef Bones, Bar B Qued, Lenny the Lifer 4.95
Little Isidore's Chopped Sirloin Steak, Sauce Large 5.95
Steak Tartar, Big Bob the Safe Opener, with Toast Points and a small bit of caviar 6.95
Beef Stroganon, which is not an "off", but is steak chunks fixed with onions, potatoes and sour cream 6.95
Steak! Which is prepared somewhat as if for Miss Diane the Hoofer with onions, mushrooms, just a pinch of garlic, flamed in cognac that is from across the drink 7.95
Rodst Prime Ribs of Very Prime Beef
   Emerald Em's Cut 7.50   Fats Feinstein's Cut 8.50
Filet Mignon, Dave the Dude 8.95
Sirloin Steak, Honolulu How, which is Prime and for "Right Guys" as well as all kinds of "Dolls" 9.50
Chateaubriand, Big Eddie's, surrounded and amid a bouquet of mostly fresh vegetables 17.95

Entrées, Which Means the Main Event

Roast Duckling with Wild Cherry Sauce, as ordered by Miss Sarah the Thrush on the occasion of the release of The Delicate Dane 6.95
Slow McCool's Marinated Baby Back Ribs, with an Ethical and Legal Sauce 6.95
Some Crepes of Young Chicken; Sauce, Nicely-Nicely 5.95
Chicken Livers with Wine and Water Chestnuts Mr. G., with Hot House Charlotte's Wild Rice 5.95
Capon a la Queen in a Pastry Shell, which is a good bet 4.95
Veal, Black Mike from Milan, which is made from very young calves of whom it is said only drink milk and do not eat very much else, and is fixed with lemon butter, some Capers and a lone Anchovy and perhaps a tiny bit of Caviar, which is not from across 7.95
Irish Hymie's Double Rib Lamb Chops with Mint Jelly 7.95
Also One Dish which is Wild Game and very exotic and is served when available and at a price which is a square rattle.

$$

Fanny's is one of the best places I know of for family dining. When it comes to spaghetti, which all kids love, there is no such thing as portion control at Fanny's. Everything that comes out of the kitchen is fresh, from vegetables to seafood. Fanny boasts that hundreds of pounds of butter are used daily in preparation of her dishes and garlic bread. Her foods are rich and bountiful. Fanny's serves some of the best fried chicken I have found anywhere. The meat practically falls from the bones. It has a savory flavor unlike anything I have tasted. Spaghetti sauces tend to be rich. Fanny's is not for the weight-conscious diner, although there is a fruit salad platter available for calorie counters. But Fanny's is best appreciated with a hearty appetite for lots of good Italian-style food. There's nothing modest or shy about Fanny, nor is there anything skimpy about her food.

FANNY'S, 1601 Simpson Street, Evanston. Telephone: GR5-8686; Chicago number, BR3-3344. Hours: 5 pm-9 pm, Monday-Friday; until 9:30 pm Saturday; noon-8 pm, Sunday. Cards: AE, BA, CB, DC, MC. Reservations suggested. Free parking in adjacent lot. Full bar service.

All Dinners include

Buttered Garlic Toast or Plain Buttered Toast, tossed Salad with Fanny's Famous Dressing, Sanka, Coffee, Tea or Milk

FANNY'S WORLD FAMOUS SPAGHETTI	3.95
MUSHROOM SPAGHETTI (no meat)	3.95
MOSTACCIOLI Served with Fanny's Spaghetti Sauce	3.95
FETTUCINI (Buttered Noodles with Cheese and Cream)	4.50
FANNY'S HOMEMADE RAVIOLI (Stuffed with Spinach, Chicken, Beef, Herbs, etc.)	4.35
FETTUCINI with Fanny's Spaghetti Sauce	4.50
FANNY'S HOMEMADE LASAGNA	4.65
FANNY'S FAMOUS SPAGHETTI With $\frac{1}{4}$ Southern Fried Chicken	4.95
With $\frac{1}{2}$ Southern Fried Chicken	5.95
SOUTHERN FRIED CHICKEN ($\frac{1}{4}$), French Fries	4.65
SOUTHERN FRIED CHICKEN ($\frac{1}{2}$), French Fries	5.25
SOUTHERN FRIED CHICKEN ($\frac{1}{4}$), With FANNY'S FETTUCINI	5.50
SOUTHERN FRIED CHICKEN ($\frac{1}{2}$), With FANNY'S FETTUCINI	6.10
FANNY'S OWN CREATION ($\frac{1}{4}$ Broiled Chicken Prepared with Fragrant Herbs, etc.) Served with Fanny's Famous Spaghetti	4.95
BROILED CHICKEN ($\frac{1}{2}$) with Fanny's Famous Spaghetti	5.95
BROILED CHICKEN ($\frac{1}{4}$) with Fettucini	5.50
BROILED CHICKEN ($\frac{1}{2}$) with Fettucini	6.10
DELUXE FRUIT PLATE (all fresh fruits) with Rouquefort, Cottage Cheese, Sesame crackers, and beverage	4.50
FRESH LAKE SUPERIOR WHITEFISH Served with Fanny's Spaghetti	5.95
FRESH LAKE SUPERIOR WHITEFISH Served with Fanny's Fettucini	6.10

Fish flown daily to Johnsen's Fish Market, Evanston — where Fanny selects and purchases it every day.

Broiled Top Prime Steaks

SIRLOIN STEAK	7.95
FILET MIGNON	7.95
PORTERHOUSE STEAK 1½ lb.	9.50
BUTTERFLY FILET MIGNON (Small Filet)	6.50
VEAL PARMIGIANA	6.50

The above steaks served with Fanny's Spaghetti or French Fries (or Baked Potato,) Salad, Delicious Garlic Bread, Coffee, Tea, Milk or Sanka

CHOPPED SIRLOIN STEAK with French Fries, Salad, Garlic Bread and Coffee, Tea, Milk or Sanka	4.65
CHOPPED SIRLOIN STEAK with Spaghetti, Salad, Garlic Bread and Coffee, Tea, Milk or Sanka	5.35
CHOPPED SIRLOIN STEAK PARMIGIANA WITH SPAGHETTI, Salad, Garlic Bread and Coffee, Tea, Milk or Sanka	5.95
CHOPPED SIRLOIN STEAK PARMIGIANA with French Fries, Garlic Bread, Salad and Coffee, Tea, Milk or Sanka	5.75

Two Delicious New Fanny Specialties

BONELESS BREAST OF CHICKEN PARMESAN	BONELESS BREAST OF CHICKEN
with Spaghetti or Potatoes Salad, Garlic Bread & Coffee, Tea, Milk or Sanka	with Marsala Wine, Cream Sauce & Fresh Mushrooms, Spaghetti or Potatoes Salad, Garlic Bread & Coffee, Tea, Milk or Sanka
5.75	5.95

FRENCH ROQUEFORT CHOPPED SIRLOIN STEAK	6.50
Served with French Fries, Salad, Garlic Bread and Coffee, Tea, Milk or Sanka	
FRENCH ROQUEFORT CHOPPED STEAK	6.95
With Fanny's Spaghetti, Garlic Bread, Salad and Coffee, Tea, Milk or Sanka	

Orland Park
FARMER'S DAUGHTER
Continental

$$

Here is the best spot in the South West suburbs for continental dining. Despite its name, there is very little that is country-kitchen about this place; the atmosphere is bright and cheery in a semisophisticated sort of way, with high ceilings and lots of open space. The special soups are always good, especially cheddar cheese. You may be tempted to order a sausage tree for an appetizer; don't do it unless you have a giant appetite. Dinners are uniformly superb. Desserts can be exceptional; I like the green apple pie and the pecan pie.

FARMER'S DAUGHTER, 14455 LaGrange Road, Orland Park. Telephone: 349-2330. Hours: 5 pm-10:30 pm, Monday-Thursday; until 11 pm Friday and Saturday; 2 pm-8 pm, Sunday. Cards: AE, BA, CB, DC, MC. Reservations required. Free parking in adjacent lot. Full bar service.

Entrees

BEEF STEAK ALA VIENNOISE 4.95
with Bordelaise Sauce and Parmesan Tomato

OUR FARMER'S DAUGHTER BAKED CHICKEN 5.95
with Old Fashioned Bread Dumpling and White Wine Sauce

WIENER SCHNITZEL 7.95
A Tender Cutlet of Selected Veal Breaded in Eggs and Milk and
Pan Fried. Topped with Fresh Lemon Slices

FILET MIGNON 8.95
The Queen of Steaks

BONELESS BREAST OF CHICKEN KIEV 7.95
Laced and Seasoned with Butter and Served on Wild and White Rice

FILET AU POIVRE 8.95
Medallions of Tenderloin Flambé in Cognac, Whole Pepper,
Sour Cream and Spices. Served with Artichoke Heart in Hollandaise
Sauce. An Award Winning Recipe From France

BEEF STROGANOFF 7.95
Top Prime Beef, Sauteed in Bordelaise Sauce, Burgundy Wine,
Fresh Mushrooms, French Garlic Spices and Sour Cream.
Served with Homemade Spaetzles

VEAL KATSU 7.95
The Farmer's Daughter Goes Japanese — Tenderloin of Milk Fed Veal,
Sprinkled with Japanese Spices, Breading and Pan Fried. Served with
Katsu Sauce and Lemon Wedges, In a Japanese Art Plate

BREAST OF CHICKEN CORDON BLEU 7.95
Stuffed with Canadian Bacon, Swiss Cheese, Spiced Butter and Topped
with Our French White Wine Sauce. Served on Wild and White Rice

PRIME RIB OF BLACK ANGUS BEEF 8.95

TENDERLOIN TIPS OF BEEF, BOURGUIGNONNE 7.95
A French Country Delight. Bordelaise Sauce

TOURNEDOS DIJON 8.95
Broiled Prime Filet Medallions, in a French Dijon Mustard and Bordelaise
Wine Sauce. Served with Artichoke Heart in Hollandaise Sauce

PRIME RIB SAN JUAN 8.95
From the Caribbean Island . . . Our Black Angus Rib Sprinkled with Salt,
Pepper, Worcestershire Sauce, a Touch of Fresh Garlic and Lightly Broiled

BRAISED SHORTRIBS-NEW ORLEANS 7.95
In Burgundy Wine Sauce, Shallots, Sliced Cucumbers and Pimentos.
Pirate Jean Lafitte Brought This Recipe From Haiti

LONDON BROIL 8.95
Prime Tenderloin Medallions, Broiled, Sliced and Covered with Bordelaise
Sauce. Served with Parmesan Tomato and Asparagus Spears in
Hollandaise Sauce

Seafood Entrees

When Your Fisherman Comes Home Without a Catch Try One of These. And We Do Like to Boast That All Our
Fish are Freshly Caught and Sometimes Throughout the Year We Will Be Unable to Obtain Some of Them

FRESH RED SNAPPER 8.75
In Hollandaise Sauce, Topped with Crisp Brown Almonds

DOVER SOLE 8.95
Rushed on Ice to Us. Boned At Your Table and Served with
Roasted Brown Almonds

SHRIMP DE JONGHE 7.95
Baked in Spiced Butter and Served in a Coquille Shell

STUFFED FILLET OF FLOUNDER 7.95
Fully Boned Flounder Fillets, Filled with Our Chef's Special Mixture of
Fresh Crab Meat, Chopped Vegetables and Just the Right Spices

FRENCH POACHED DOVER SOLE 8.95
Boned to Fillets and Poached in a French White Wine and Vegetables.
Served with a Delightful Hollandaise Sauce

KANDY'S SPECIAL 8.50
Icelandic Fillet of Turbot, Flown to Us Via Air Canada. Dipped in Our
Own Beer Batter and Pan Fried to a Golden Crispness. Served with Our
Tartar Relish Sauce and Lemon Wedges

Oak Brook
FOND DE LA TOUR
French
$$$

For businesspeople or others in the Oak Brook area who
want to entertain in a fine French atmosphere, Fond de la
Tour is the only choice. It also happens to be a good
restaurant under any circumstances. There are seats for 72
people in the intimate dining room. Plans call for addition
of at least three private dining rooms to accommodate
another dozen people each. Best selections from the à la
carte menu include extraordinary rack of lamb for two,
superb steak Madagascar in a green peppercorn sauce and

Les Poissons

QUENELLE DE HOMMARD 9.25
Mousse of lobster with sauce Americaine

SOLE DE DOUVRE A LA MEUNIERE 8.75
Dover sole sauteed in butter, lemon and parsley

CREVETTES DE JONGHE 8.00
Jumbo shrimp baked in a crust of garlic flavored fresh bread crumbs

QUEUES D'HOMMARD GRILLEES . . . . Market Price
Broiled lobster tails served with drawn butter

POISSON ROUGE A LA PROVENCALE 8.50
Red snapper baked in a country sauce

TURBOT DUGLERE 8.75
Turbot braised in white wine and tomato flavored Duglere sauce

CUISSES DE GRENOUILLES PROVENCALE 8.50
Frog legs sauteed in butter, shallots, tomamto and a hint of garlic

Les Entrees

POULET SAUTE AU VINAIGRE 8.50
Chicken sauteed with tomato - garlic, and bordelaise sauce
topped with fresh butter

CANETON A LA BIGARADE 8.75
Oven crisp roast duckling with orange sauce, served with wild rice

EMINCE DE BOEUF, BORDELAISE 8.75
Beef tenderloin sauteed and served in bordelaise sauce

RIS DE VEAU NOILLY PRATT 9.00
Sweetbreads poached and sauteed in butter, flavored with vermouth

BOEUF EN BROCHETTE FLAMBEE 8.75
Cubes of marinated beef tenderloin, onion, bacon, green pepper and
mushroom, served with wild rice

excellent roast duck in an orange and flamed brandy sauce. Many dishes are beautifully prepared tableside. Wines are reasonably priced although the list does not include vintage designation.

FOND DE LA TOUR, 40 North Tower Road, Oak Brook. Telephone: 620-1500. Lunch: 11:30 am-2:30 pm, Tuesday-Friday. Dinner: 6 pm-midnight, Tuesday-Saturday; 4 pm-10 pm, Sunday; closed Monday. Cards: AE, BA, DC, MC. Reservations required. Valet parking. Full bar service.

ESCALOPES DE VEAU AU MARSALA 9.00
*Thin slices of veal sauteed at your table and finished with a
light marsala wine sauce, served with white rice*

CARRE D'AGNEAU PROVENCALE .... (each) 10.75
*Roast rack of spring lamb, finished in a crust of seasoned bread crumbs,
lightly touched with garlic.
Served with an assortment of freshly cooked vegetables, (for two or more)*

STEAK DIANE 10.50
Mignonettes of beef seasoned and flamed at your table

Les Grillades

TOURNEDOS ROSSINI 10.75
Twin filet mignons served with pate de fois gras on toasted croutons

FILET MIGNON GRILLE BEARNAISE 10.50
*Center cut of tenderloin served with bearnaise sauce,
accompanied by mushroom caps and broiled tomato*

ENTRECOTE AMERICAINE GRILLE 9.75
*Broiled strip sirloin with tomato and mushrooms, served with sauce bearnaise,
and selection of fresh cooked vegetables*

STEAK AU POIVRE 10.75
*Tender filet with freshly crushed peppercorns, sauteed and
flamed at your table with brandy*

ENTRECOTE AU POIVRE VERT 10.50
Broiled strip sirloin served with a sauce of Madagascar green peppercorns

CHATEAUBRIAND AUX CHAMPIGNONS .... (each) 10.75
*Broiled double tenderloin with mushroom caps and bearnaise,
sliced at tableside and served with an array of fresh vegetable,
(for two or more)*

FILET DE BOEUF EN CROUTE...................... (each) 12.00
*Tenderloin encased with pate de foie gras and flakey pastry crust,
served with sauce perigourdine
(for two or more)*

Chicago
FOUR TORCHES
American

$$

A sometime hangout for celebrities, Four Torches deserves more attention from the general restaurant-going public than it gets. Although its North Side location is off the beaten path, Four Torches is well worth the short cab ride from the Loop, or even a drive from the suburbs. The restaurant has a low-key sophistication about it, but you may hear an occasional staccato laugh leap out from the cocktail lounge. The food at first glance appears to be basic American, but do not overlook the pleasant Greek accents which abound. For instance, beef citron combines flavors you might not think of as compatible, but which work well. I also like the pepper steak, which, as the menu points out, is highly seasoned; this one is not for the timid. Four Torches seafood is always fresh, except, of course, for imports. And how can you find fault with any restaurant that warns against well-done steaks?

FOUR TORCHES, 1960 North Lincoln Park West, Chicago. Telephone: 248-5505. Hours: 5 pm-1 am, Monday-Thursday; until 1:30 am Friday; until 2:30 am Saturday; until midnight Sunday. Cards: AE, BA, CB, MC. Reservations suggested. Parking in building. Full bar service; wine list limited.

Four Torches SPECIALTIES

BEEF CITRON—Slices of Tenderloin,
  served on a mound of rice, flavored with
  a delicate lemon sauce. French green beans   8.50

BEEF COLBERT, Beef Tenderloin on Wild Rice
  prepared in a delicate wine sauce   9.25

PEPPER STEAK, Served with Consommè Rice   8.25

LOBSTER BROCHETTE
  Served on a Mound of Rice Pilaf   8.75

TENDERLOIN STEAK, EN BROCHETTE
  Prime Tenderloin on a Flaming Dagger
  Served with Rice Pilaf   7.25

VEAL PICCANTE, Served with Sauted Green Peppers
  or French Green Beans   9.25

THE PEPPERCORN STEAK, Broiled Sliced Heart of Sirloin
  —A highly seasoned Specialty of the House,
  Served with Green Beans Almondine   9.25

BROILED BABY CALVES LIVER, served with
  Burmuda Onions or Bacon. Baked Potato   7.50

ALL THE ABOVE SERVED WITH SALAD:
FRENCH, GARLIC OR THOUSAND ISLAND DRESSING

FROM OUR CHARCOAL HEARTH

NEW YORK CUT SIRLOIN STEAK
  15 Oz. prime center cut Sirloin, dry-aged
  and broiled to perfection   10.50
NEW YORK PEPPERCORN STEAK
  Served with French Cut Green Beans   10.50
NEW YORK CRUMB STEAK
  Served with Green Peppers   10.50
BROILED FILET MIGNON—10 Oz.   9.25
TOP SIRLOIN BUTT STEAK—12 Oz.
  Large Prime Center Cut Butt Steak
  Broiled to Your Individual Taste   9.50

Chicago
FRENCH PORT
Seafood

$$

What visions the words "French port" create in the mind's eye! Fishermen of Brittany hauling in their nets; a steamy waterfront dive in Marseilles. This French Port offers cozy dining in surroundings of polished plank-topped tables or booths and lath and plaster wall decor. The dinner menu consists almost entirely of fresh fish, in most cases prepared simply over a charcoal broiler with nothing added to detract from their natural goodness. There is also the obligatory steak for confirmed carnivores, plus duck à l'orange, chicken and veal Madeira. On Thursdays only, French Port serves couscous, the Moroccan staple of millet, vegetables and seasonings. Couscous is served either vegetarian-style or with lamb. The luncheon menu is quite reasonable and includes various crêpes, omelettes, fried fish and burgers.

FRENCH PORT, 2585 North Clark Street, Chicago. Telephone: 528-6644. Lunch: 11 am-4 pm, Wednesday-Monday. Dinner: 4 pm-11 pm, Monday, Wednesday and Thursday; until midnight Friday and Saturday; until 11 pm Sunday; closed Tuesday. Cards: MC. Reservations suggested. Free parking garage just to the south on North Clark Street. Full bar service.

French Port

ENTRÉES DE LA MER

Fillet of Herring Almondine	5.25
Lobster Tail	9.00
Crab Legs	8.00
African Frog Legs	7.75
Stuffed Flounder	6.75
Stuffed Lake Trout	7.75
Stuffed Walleye Pike	7.75
Salmon en Façon Viennesse	7.00
Mullet en Papillote	6.75
Poisson en Croûte	7.75
Sea Trout Provençal	6.75
White Fish Fillet	6.25
Squid Français	4.75
Shrimp Oregano	6.25

FRESH WHOLE BROILED FISH

Red Snapper	6.50
Flounder	5.75
Sea Bass	5.75
Mackerel	4.50
Monk Fish	5.75
Black Snapper	5.25
Whiting Fish	4.00

ENTRÉES SPECIAL

8 oz. Fillet Mignon	7.50
Brochette	5.75

Chicago
GARDEN OF HAPPINESS
Korean $$

If you like to charcoal broil your steaks in the backyard, chances are you'll love Korean food. Not that Korea is a nation of backyard barbecuers, but grilled meats make up a delightful part of that Asian nation's cuisine. Garden of Happiness features both Chinese and Korean foods, but it is known mostly for the latter. In fact, it is a local nightspot of some renown among the Chicago Korean community—a good sign of authenticity. You can order several items à la carte or save some money by trying the special dinner. In either case, don't miss charcoal-broiled short ribs of beef, or fire meat, slices of beef marinated and grilled. Kim chee, as characteristic of Korean meals as is lettuce and tomatoes of American, is a spicy hot marinated cabbage that goes well with the meat. For meat and mixed vegetable fanciers, try san juk. Red snapper in hot sauce should satisfy the fish lovers at your table. Don't miss the spun sugar-glazed fruit for dessert. Go with a number of friends to try lots of different foods.

GARDEN OF HAPPINESS, 3450 North Lincoln Avenue, Chicago. Telephone: 348-2120. Hours: 11 am-midnight, daily. Cards: AE, CB, MC. Reservations suggested. Street parking. Full bar service.

KOREAN FOODS

FIRE MEAT
Slices of Sirloin Beef Marinated in Special Korean
Sauce and Charcoal Broiled   3.75

SHORT RIBS
Selected Tender Short Ribs Marinated in Korean
Sauce and Charcoal Broiled   3.75

SAN JUK
Sliced Sirloin Beef Marinated in Special Sauce
interlaced with mushrooms, greenpeppers,
scallions, tomatoes and charcoal broiled   4.25

DAHK BOKEM
Sauteed Chicken in Korean Sauce with Vegetable   3.25

CHOP CHAE
Threaded vegetables sauteed with Beef and Mixed
Vermicelli   2.95

SHRIMP TEMPURA
Deep fried Indian Jumbo Shrimps and Vegetables   4.75

RED SNAPPER
Marinated in Special Sauce and Deep Fried   6.50
                                                              8.50

BI BEAM BOP
Steamed Rice Topped with Namool (vegetables)
Fire Meat Fried Egg and Special Hot sauce   2.95

BUCK WHEAT NOODLE
in Cold Broth or Hot Broth and Topped with
Pickle Kimchee   2.95
Beef   6.50
Boiled Egg   3.25

GAYLORD INDIA RESTAURANT
Indian

$$

Gaylord India Restaurant offers the best Indian cooking available in Chicago. Though far from what we usually think of as a chain restaurant, it is part of an international chain with branches in India, London, New York and San Francisco. There are scores of cooking styles in the large and populous subcontinent of India. At Gaylord we get a taste of the northern cuisine, characterized by tandoori cooking. The tandoors are deep clay-lined pits embedded in a tile-covered counter. Each holds a bed of white-hot charcoal over which long-marinated meats are quickly cooked to seal in flavor and juices. When roasted in the tandoor, chicken or lamb, covered with a red-colored, yogurt-based marinade, take on a complex charcoal taste that you just can't capture in your backyard barbecue. No beef is served because of the Hindu taboo, but delicious chicken, lamb, prawns and vegetarian dishes are regular menu items. Naturally, vegetables are handled in an outstanding way, some spicy, others mild. Combination platters offer beginners a good assortment of textures and tastes. At the end of your meal take hot tea and any of the refreshingly sweet desserts. Wines are available, but beer is preferable with curries.

GAYLORD INDIA RESTAURANT, 678 North Clark, Chicago. Telephone: 664-1700. Lunch: 11:30 am-2:30 pm, Monday-Friday. Dinner: 5:30 pm-10:30 pm, Sunday-Friday; until 11 pm Saturday. Cards: AE, BA, CB, DC, MC. Reservations suggested. Free parking lot across street. Full bar service.

Tandoori Specialities

Chicken *(Chicken marinated in spices and cooked on charcoal in a clay oven)*   Full 5.00   Half 2.75
Boti Kabab *(Cubed leg of lamb roasted on a skewer)* 3.75
Seikh Kabab *(Minced lamb mixed with onions and herbs and roasted on skewers)* 3.75
Chicken Tikka Kabab *(Boneless chicken pieces roasted Tandoori style)* 3.50
Tandoori Prawns *(King prawns roasted in tandoori)* 3.95

Vegetarian

Mattar Paneer *(Green peas cooked in home made cheese)* 2.75
Chana Masaladar *(Chic peas cooked in spices)* 2.75
Kofta Paneer *(Home made cheese chunks spiced and fried and cooked in a delicious gravy)* 2.75
Alu Gobbi Masala *(Potatoes and cauliflower, cooked with herbs and spices)* 2.75
Dal Special *(Creamed lentils)* 2.75
Bhindi *(Fried okra)* 2.75
Sag Paneer *(Creamed spinach and home made cheese cooked in spices)* 2.75
Alu Bengan *(Egg plant and potato)* 2.75
Alu Raita *(Old fashioned yoghurt and potatoes and cucumber flavoured with mint leaves)* 2.75
Sukhi Dal *(Lentils delicately spiced)* 2.75
Vegetables mixed

Chicago
GENE & GEORGETTI
Steaks/Italian

$$

Sad to say, but Chicago has few restaurants left that can be described as institutions. The London House is no more, nor is The Stockyard Inn. But Gene & Georgetti continues strong on a fast track. A masculine kind of restaurant sans locker room ambience, Gene & Georgetti is a headquarters for fans of real Chicago-style beefsteak. Served without embellishment or seasonings, steaks come straight from broiler to table. Ask for a garlic rub or salt and pepper to taste at the table and you'll get perfect satisfaction. Don't ignore the Italian specialties. Sauces are Tuscan, yielding a meaty flavor with less tomato acidity. The veal Parmigiana is mouth-watering. Pastas are served family-style; the

Steaks and Chops
We Serve Aged Prime Beef Exclusively

Broiled Filet Mignon	$11.50
Broiled Sirloin Steak	11.50
Broiled Strip Sirloin	11.50
Broiled T-Bone Steak	13.50
Broiled Small Steak	9.95
Pepper Steak	8.50
Broiled Lamb Chops	11.50
Broiled Pork Chops	7.50

Spaghetti and Ravioli

Canelloni	$5.25
Ravioli With Meat Sauce	4.50
Spaghetti With Meat Sauce	4.50
Spaghetti a La Marinara	4.50
Spaghetti L' Acciughe	4.50
Spaghetti Al Burro	4.50
Spaghetti With Mushroom Sauce	4.75
Spaghetti With Meat Balls	4.75
Mostaccioli With Meat Sauce	4.75
Linguini White Clam Sauce	5.75
Spaghetti White Clam Sauce	5.75

linguini in white clam sauce is especially excellent. More standard fare is also available, including whitefish, chicken, duck and calf's liver. A small selection of wines complements a full bar. Gene & Georgetti is a favorite not only of Chicago cognoscenti, but attracts hordes of commercial visitors drawn by the nearby Merchandise Mart and new Wolf Point Apparel Mart.

GENE & GEORGETTI, 500 North Franklin Street, Chicago. Telephone: 527-3718. Hours: 11 am-midnight, Monday-Saturday; closed Sunday. Cards: AE. Reservations accepted. Ample free parking. Full bar service.

Entrees

Calf's Liver and Bacon	$6.75
Chopped Sirloin Steak	5.75
Half Spring Chicken (Broiled or Fried)	5.75
Beef En Brochette	8.50

Italian Specialties

Chicken Cacciatora	$6.50
Chicken Vesuvio	6.50
Chicken Florentine Style	6.50
Veal Scaloppine	6.25
Veal Florentine	6.25
Veal Cutlet Parmigiana	6.25
Breaded Veal Cutlet	6.00

Sea Foods

Lobster Tail	$11.25
Lobster Tail De Jonge	11.50
Lobster a La Diavolo	11.50
Whitefish	8.50
Shrimps De Jonge	7.00
French Fried Shrimps	7.00

Chicago
GENESEE DEPOT
American

$

Stepping inside this tiny storefront restaurant is like visiting a country kitchen of 50 or 60 years ago. Brick, bare wood and quaint floral paper adorn the walls. There are only nine tables, each graced with fresh flowers. You would be hard-pressed to spend more than $10 per couple for dinner. There are no printed menus; instead a menu card posted near the front door lists the three daily specialties. Dinner items are rotated regularly from a selection of about 15 or so entrées. Among the choices are Greenland turbot stuffed with breading, mushrooms and parsley, beef stroganoff and stuffed Cornish hen. The hen, by the way, is roasted with a whole orange in its abdominal cavity and is served with long-grain and wild rice. Other choices might include red snapper Creole, brisket of beef or boned chicken breast in white wine sauce. These dinners, priced from $3.75 to $4.50, include homebaked bread, soup of the day or salad and appropriate side vegetables. Desserts are $1 to $1.25 extra, all homemade.

GENESEE DEPOT, 3736 North Broadway, Chicago. Telephone: 528-6990. Hours: 5:30 pm-9:30 pm, Wednesday-Sunday; closed Monday and Tuesday. No cards. No reservations. No alcoholic beverages; you may bring your own wine selection.

Chicago
GINO'S EAST
Italian

$

A place popular with college kids, hospital technicians and secretaries, Gino's East just happens to have some of the best pizza around. It is Chicago-style pizza, deep dish with a thick, almost cake-crumb crust, rich pizza sauce and gobs of toppings over cheese. If something other than pizza is your choice, pasta dishes are most satisfying; I particularly enjoy green noodles with meatballs. There are two dining rooms served by the same kitchen. One is downstairs, a grotto-like affair with wooded tables and bench seating. The upstairs dining room has a gracious white-tablecloth setting. Take your pick, depending on how you are dressed and what mood suits you. By the way, you can stick with the house wines by C-K Mondavi and not go wrong.

GINO'S EAST, 160 East Superior, Chicago. Telephone: 943-1124. Hours: 11 am-2 am, Monday-Saturday; 4 pm-2 am, Sunday (pizza ovens shut down nightly at 1 am). Cards: AE. Reservations suggested. Parking in city garage nearby. Full bar service.

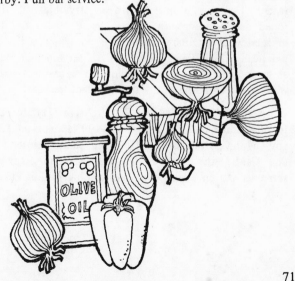

Forest Park
GIANNOTTI'S
Italian

$$

This is one of the best, if not the absolute best, Italian restaurants in the United States. Giannotti's seats over 200 people, but the personal touch has not been lost in service or presentation. Seven-course dinners are specialties, as is the "family fiesta dinner" for four or more people at $8.75. Dinners include soup, salad, pasta, entrée, dessert and coffee. Of the entrées, my favorite is the veal piccante, the finest served anywhere. Baby veal is sautéed in butter and served in a lemon-butter sauce with bits of pine nuts as a topping. But don't overlook the à la carte treats. Among dinner preludes, stuffed mushrooms, baked clams and black mussels are all topnotch. Merluzzi, a cold salad of white fish in olive oil with olives and pimientos, is in a class by itself. Pastas are all homemade, prepared perfectly and served with sauces that have been simmered for hours. Specialty vegetables are not always listed on the menu; ask what is available for the day. You might enjoy fried cauliflower patties or the most sensational eggplant dish you have ever tasted. The pulp is beaten into a patty, breaded, fried, rolled and stuffed with ricotta cheese, baked and then drizzled with marinara sauce. It is so light and fluffy it practically floats from the platter. Desserts include Italian anise cookies and creamy, mellow cheesecake, as well as watermelon and other fruits at all times of the year.

GIANNOTTI'S ITALIAN RESTAURANT, 7711 Roosevelt Road, Forest Park. Telephone: 366-1199. Hours: 4pm-12:30 am, Tuesday-Saturday; 2 pm-10:30 pm, Sunday; closed Monday. Cards: AE, CB, DC. Reservations required (may be some waiting on weekends). Valet parking. Full bar service.

Giannotti's table d'Hote Dinner

7 Course Dinners include: Soup — Our Own Special Salad with choice of your favorite Dressing
(our Olive Oil and Vinegar, French, Garlic or 1000 Island — Roquefort Dressing 50c extra)
Side Order of Mostaccioli or Ravioli — Assorted Cookies — Fruit — Coffee or Tea

Steaks and Chops from the Broiler

Not Responsible For Well Done Steaks

PRIME NEW YORK CUT SIRLOIN STEAK 10.75
FILET MIGNON 10.75
PRIME RIB EYE STEAK 10.75
LADIES CUT PRIME SIRLOIN STEAK 9.75
PEPPER STEAK 8.50
DOUBLE THICK LAMB CHOPS or Thin (3) 8.50
CENTER CUT PORK CHOPS 7.75
CHOPPED SIRLOIN 5.50
BRAGIOLE A LA NAPOLITANA Rolled Butt 'Steak with our Special Seasoning 7.00
PRIME STEAK A LA PIZZAIOLO 11.75
Prime New York Cut Sirloin Saute in Olive Oil, Fresh Tomatoes and Oregano

Veal Dishes

VEAL PICCANTE 7.50
Sliced Veal sauted in Butter and Lemon with a Special Topping
VEAL SCALOPPINE 7.50
Sliced Veal Steak, sauted in Tomato Sauce, White Wine and fresh Mushrooms
VEAL PARMIGIANA 7.50
VEAL FRANCAISE 7.50
Patties of Veal dipped in Flour and Egg, fried in Butter, Lemon Rings
BREADED VEAL CUTLET 7.50
VEAL SCALOPPINE MARSALA Sliced Veal Steak, sauted in Butter, Marsala Wine 7.50
VEAL SALTIMBOCCA A LA PARMIGIANA 7.50
Sliced Veal Cutlet, stuffed with Prosciutto and covered with Cheese and Baked
VEAL SCALOPPINE A LA GIANNOTTI 7.50
Sliced Veal, sauted in Butter, White Wine, Fresh Mushrooms, Onions, and Fresh Green Peppers

Poultry

BONELESS CHICKEN A LA PARMIGIANA 7.00
BONELESS CHICKEN FRANCAISE 7.00
CHICKEN A LA CACCIATORE 7.00
Chicken, sauted in Olive Oil, White Wine, Fresh Tomatoes, Mushrooms
CHICKEN VESUVIO Chicken, sauted in Olive Oil, Garlic, Oregano, White Wine 7.00
CHICKEN A LA FLORENTINA Chicken, dipped in Egg Batter, fried in Olive Oil 7.00
PLATTER OF CHICKEN LIVER, Mushroom Sauce 6.25
CHICKEN OREGANATO Chicken, sauted in Butter, Lemon, Oregano 7.00

Seafood

COMBINATION LOBSTER AND FILET 12.50
BROILED AFRICAN LOBSTER with Melted Butter 13.75
BROILED RED SNAPPER, Almondine Sauce 7.50
BROILED DOVER SOLE with Almondine Sauce 10.75
FRENCH FRIED SHRIMP 7.50
SHRIMP MARINARA SAUCE 7.50
ZUPPA DI PESCE A LA NAPOLITANA with Linguini 10.50
BAKED BACCALA — Cod Fish 6.50
CALAMARI (Baby Squid) With Linguini or Spaghetti 6.25
LOBSTER FRA DIAVOLO 13.75
Lobster tail, sauted in Tomato, White Wine, served over Linguini or Spaghetti

Chicago
GRANDMA'S RECEIPTS
American

$$

Chances are your grandma was not a gourmet; more likely she cooked up good, sturdy fare that sent you back to the serving platter for seconds. Don't demand more of Grandma's Receipts than it is. It is not the ultimate in haute cuisine; it is a colorful and inexpensive restaurant where the portions are filling and the food is pleasing. The atmosphere suggests yesteryear rural America. The ceiling is cluttered with some 75 or more Tiffany lamps. Floors are wood-pegged. Walls are rough-wooded barn board. The menu makes no attempt at anything more exotic than spaghetti and meatballs. But everything is freshly cooked. Some desserts, such as a serving of apple pie large enough for two people, are exceptional. What can you say about chicken and dumplings? Though not outstanding, it is good. The chicken comes in a creamy sauce with two dumplings the size of tennis balls. Sandwiches are available for smaller appetites.

GRANDMA'S RECEIPTS, 2837 North Clark Street, Chicago. Telephone: 528-2249. Hours: 11am-10 pm, Sunday-Thursday; until 11 pm Friday and Saturday. Cards: AE, BA, DC. Reservations accepted. Street parking difficult; garages nearby. Full bar service.

Chicago
GREAT GRITZBE'S
American/International

$$

One of the most original restaurant ideas since tables and chairs, GGFFS is another project of Lettuce Entertain You, Inc. (see R.J. Grunts and Lawrence of Oregano)—lots of imaginative surroundings, unusual drinks, a cheese and dessert bar plus lots of good food. Most evenings will require a wait in the cocktail lounge where you can nibble on cheese and crackers. The lounge has what appears to be a random placement of large blocks in a stair step arrangement climbing one wall, making an indoor bleachers on which to sit and pass the time. Some recommendations from Gritzbe's large menu: Chicken teriyaki is plump and sweet. Veal Leroy stands out as does the reasonably priced duck. If you feel like something very rich, try the lobster Benedict or "the French toast connection." Lots of salads will make vegetarians happy. The dessert bar is a non-dieter's paradise.

GREAT GRITZBE'S FLYING FOOD SHOW, 21 East Chestnut, Chicago. Telephone: 642-3460. Hours: 11:30 am-midnight, Monday-Thursday; until 1 am Friday and Saturday; 10 am-midnight, Sunday. Sunday brunch: 10 am-2 pm. No cards. No reservations. Plenty of nearby garage parking. Full bar service.

GREEK ISLANDS

$$

The partisan rivalry between supporters of the Greek res-
taurants in Chicago may be even more intense than the
rivalry between White Sox and Cubs fans. The restaurants
proudly advertise their support, plastering windows with
endorsements, photographs and letters from adoring pa-
trons. It would be impossible for any Greek restaurant to
live up 100 percent to such praise, but they all keep trying.
There is probably no Greek restaurant in Chicago with as
vocal a following as Greek Islands. I understand the enthu-
siasm, but the place is not without its flaws. There is,
however, plenty of good food at reasonable prices. Service
is topnotch and the surroundings are pleasant. You will find
the usual lineup of Greek foods—braised lamb, loin and leg

SEA FOOD

A La Carte

Shrimps (Greek Style)	4.25
Broiled Sea Bass (According to Weight	
Broiled Red Snapper (According to Weight)	
Fried Squid	2.95
Fried Smelts	2.95
Hot Octopus in Wine Sauce	2.95
Cold Octopus in Vinegar Sauce	2.95
Fried Cod Fish (Bakalao) Garlic Sauce	3.15

GREEK ISLANDS SPECIALS

Family Style Taramosalata, Saganaki, Salad, Gyros, Roast Lamb, Dolmathes, Mousaka or Pastichio, Dessert and Coffee ————— per person	5.95
Gyros Plate	2.95
Combination Plate (Leg Lamb, Mousaka, Shrimp, V. Leaves, Veg. Pot.)	3.50
Stuffed Vine Leaves (Dolmades)	2.60
Mousaka (Stuffed Egg Plant)	2.75
Pastichio (Stuffed Macaroni)	2.65
Rice Pilaf with Yogourt	1.95
Spanakotiropita (Spinach-Cheese Pie)	2.60
Baked Lima Beans	1.00

Roasts

Special Loin of Lamb	3.95
Roast Leg of Lamb	3.50
Roast Leg of Lamb (Children's Portion)	2.50

From The Broiler

Broiled Lamb Chops	(2), 5.25; (3), 6.75
Broiled Greek Sausage	2.95
Broiled Pork Chops (2)	3.10
Broiled Steak - N.Y. Sirloin	6.75
Souvlaki - Shishkebab	3.50
Fried Lamb Liver and Sausage	2.95
Fried Lamb Livers	2.75

of lamb, souvlaki, pastichio and mousaka—on and on it goes. Most selections are in the $2.50 to $4 range; add $1.50 more and get the complete dinner from soup to dessert. The Greek Islands has built its biggest following on fresh seafood, particularly the red snapper and sea bass. They are priced according to weight and usually you will pay under $5 à la carte. But sometimes, as good as it can be, the fish falls short of perfection. Nevertheless, Greek Islands is worth the attention of the enterprising diner.

GREEK ISLANDS, 766 West Jackson, Chicago. Telephone: 782-9855. Hours: 11 am-midnight, Sunday-Thursday; until 2 am Friday and Saturday. Cards: AE, CB. Reservations accepted. Free parking in nearby lot. Full bar service.

DAILY SPECIALS (Possible Changes in These Specials)

A La Carte

Sunday:
Bar-B-Q Lamb	3.75
Special Beef (Moshari), with Rice or Potato	3.50
Lamb and Artichokes Avgolemono	3.25
Braised Lamb and Spaghetti	2.95

Monday:
Lamb with Vegetables, Egg Lemon (Fricassee)	2.95
Beef Stifado	3.60
Chicken Riganeti	¼, 2.25 - ½, 3.25

Tuesday:
Stuffed Peppers	2.50
Braised Lamb with Spinach	2.95
Braised Lamb Rosa Marina	2.95
Baked Bacalao	2.95

Wednesday:
Lamb and Artichokes Avgolemono	3.25
Stuffed Peppers	2.50
Baked Fish (a la Spetsiota)	3.75

Thursday:
Stuffed Peppers	2.50
Beef Stifado	3.60
Chicken Riganeti	¼, 2.25 - ½, 3.35

Friday:
Stuffed Squid	2.75
Braised Lamb with Spinach Rice (Spanocorizo)	2.95
Baked Bacalao	2.95
Baked Red Snapper (Marinato)	3.75
Bar-B-Q Lamb	3.75

Saturday:
Lamb and Artichokes Avgolemono	3.25
Braised Lamb Rosa Marina	2.95
Bar-B-Q Lamb	3.75

Chicago
HANA EAST
Japanese

$$

There is probably no display in the restaurant business like that put on by Japanese chefs at hibachi steak tables. Of several such places in the Chicago area, the best is Hana East. Japanese steak houses are deliberately tailored to American tastes. Little of the exotic in culinary fare exists here, but what is served at Hana East is delicious. You'll be seated at a large table for 10 around a central gas-heated cooking surface. Your chef for the evening works at one side of the table dicing, slicing and grilling in a digital display that is like watching a skilled magician. Order from the complete dinners and begin with an appetizer of hibachi-grilled shrimp. Next comes a small bowl of chicken broth delicately seasoned. By this time, your chef has begun work on grilling vegetables and meat, slicing with samurai-like precision, beating out a rhythmic tattoo as wooden salt and pepper shakers slam against each other like castanets. In the process, of course, your food gets properly seasoned. You could order wine to drink with dinner, but keep in the spirit of the place and order Japanese beer or warm sake instead.

HANA EAST, 210 East Ohio, Chicago. Telephone: 751-2100. Lunch: 11:30 am-2:30 pm, Monday-Friday. Dinner: 5 pm-11 pm, Monday-Thursday; until midnight Friday; until 1 am Saturday; 4 pm-11 pm, Sunday. Cards: AE, BA, CB, DC, MC. Reservations suggested. Street parking or nearby garages. Full bar service.

Dinner

Appetizer

Hibachi Shrimp

Soup

Chicken Soup Ala Japanese

Salad

Hana East Salad Bowl

Entreés

Hibachi Chicken with Fresh Vegetables	6.95
Hibachi Steak (Sirloin) with Fresh Vegetables	9.25
Filet Mignon with Fresh Vegetables	9.50
Hanayaki Steak with Fresh Vegetables	8.75
Hibachi Shrimp with Fresh Vegetables	8.50

Desserts

Ice Cream or Sherbet

Hana East Special

Chicken Soup Ala Japanese

Hibachi Shrimp

Hana East Salad Bowl

Hot Sake - Japanese wine

Hibachi Special Steak

Hibachi Vegetables
with our Special Sauce

Ice Cream or Sherbet

Plum Wine

$15.00 Per Person

Chicago
HALF SHELL
Seafood

$

This is one of those places at which you never find tourists; even many Chicagoans would have a tough time finding it. But if you want in on the secret, walk about a block west on Diversey from Clark Street, go down a few steps into a relatively small basement room and you're inside the Half Shell. About 20 bar stools, a few tables, low ceilings and an interesting menu of seafoods make up one of the more unusual restaurant settings in the city. If your bag happens to be caviar, get two ounces for $8 and wash it down with a bottle of Heidsieck Monopole for $12 more. But if your budget and tastes are more modest, two can easily dine for $10 or less. The house specialty is the Half Shell mulligan. Served in a cast metal cooking platter, it's chock full of clams, whole shrimp, perch and vegetables—all mulled together into a delicious and filling broth. The clams actually taste like the ocean smells. Plump frog legs in a crispy fried batter and mammoth Dungeness crab, the kind you dig into with your fingers and make a mess, are other favorites. For confirmed carnivores, the Turkish shishkebab may be out of place in the Half Shell but it is one of the best I've tasted in a long time. Service can sometimes be slow, but if you go with interesting people and good conversation, you'll have time to linger over drinks and appetizers.

HALF SHELL, 676 West Diversey Parkway, Chicago. Telephone: 549-1773. Hours: 11:30 am-about midnight, daily. No cards. No reservations. Parking at Century Plaza Garage north of Diversey on Clark. Full bar service.

Chicago
HOBSON'S OYSTER BAR
Seafood

$

One doesn't go to Hobson's for a demonstration of the art of interior decoration. One does go there for a sensational crab and shrimp gumbo for $1.50 a bowl, or to order a clam stew called clam LaFite for about a quarter less. Here one can get a whole Dungeness crab, moderately sized, for $5. As you might guess, Hobson's is the real thing. Located just a block or so north of Marina City, the only identification is a couple of red neon signs in the window that proclaim "Oyster Bar." Inside, the place has the character of a neighborhood bar and in fact Hobson's does draw its regulars. But passersby are just as welcome, if they can find seats or stools. Oysters and cherrystone clams are $2 per half dozen; shrimp platters and sandwiches round out the rather brief menu. But the gumbo is the thing for me here and that's no Hobson's choice.

HOBSON'S OYSTER BAR, 448 North State Street, Chicago. Telephone: DE 7-4426. Hours: 11:30 am-11:30 pm, Monday-Friday; noon-11:30 pm, Saturday; closed Sunday. Cards: AE. No reservations. Street parking. Full bar service.

Chicago
HOUSE OF BERTINI
Steaks

$$

House of Bertini has been a Chicago fixture since the 1930's and continues to be a favorite among a not-so-limited number of cognoscenti. West of the convention and business hotel district, it is a pleasant little restaurant in which to unwind and forget busier pursuits of the day. Now operated by John Rossi, grandson of the original Mr. Bertini, the restaurant boasts a menu of steaks, fish, chicken and chops with some tasty Italian additions. Steaks are particularly recommended. And, you know it's got to be good because John Rossi and his family live right upstairs.

HOUSE OF BERTINI, 535 North Wells Street, Chicago. Telephone: 644-1397. Lunch: 11:30 am-2:30 pm, Monday-Saturday. Dinner: 5 pm-11:30 pm, Monday-Saturday; closed Sunday. Cards: AE, MC. Reservations suggested (particularly weekends). Free parking after 5 pm in nearby lots. Full bar service; limited wine list.

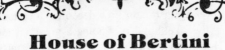

House of Bertini

Complete Dinner Menu

Appetizers (Choice of One)

Soup — Tomato Juice — Spaghetti — Shrimp Cocktail (1.00 extra)

Extra Cut T-Bone (24 oz.)	$10.00
Large T-Bone (18 oz.)	9.00
Extra Cut Sirloin (16 oz.)	8.75
Sirloin (12 oz.)	8.25
Filet Mignon (9 oz.)	8.75
Junior Filet Mignon (6 oz.)	7.75
Loin Pork Chops (2)	6.75
Loin Lamb Chops (2)	7.50
Pan Fried Chicken (½)	5.75
Chicken a la Cacciatora	6.00
Calf's Liver & Bacon	6.00
Chicken Parmigiana	6.25
Veal Parmigiana	7.75
Broiled Fresh White Fish	7.25
Sauted Veal ala Lemon	7.75

Tossed Salad — *French, Thousand Island, Oil & Vinegar or Garlic (French or Cream Roquefort - .50 extra)*
Vegetable and Cottage Fried Potatoes

Desserts & Beverages

Spumoni	Coffee
Vanilla Ice Cream	Hot Tea
Bisque Tortoni	Sanka
Chocolate Sundae	

Chicago
HOUSE OF HUNAN
Chinese (Mandarin/Hunan)

$$

Over and over again I learn how deceptive location can be in judging the likelihood of finding a great restaurant in Chicago. House of Hunan is up a steep flight of stairs on the second floor of a nondescript building just south of the busy intersection of Lincoln, Belmont and Damen. The food here is sensational. Start with plump shrimp toast and perhaps kou-te, little meat-filled steamed dumplings, as a second appetizer. Even the fried won ton are special, stuffed with a ground meat filling. A Mandarin classic, shark's fin soup, is $8 for four people. My favorite is sizzling rice soup in a double portion for $2.95. And yes, the rice really does sizzle when it is dropped into the hot steaming soup. You can choose your dinner courses from among 70 selections. Go with a group to share each course in order to savor the different tastes and textures. To enjoy the beautifully prepared and artistically served Peking duck, it's worth the $16 charge and the need to call ahead. Another outstanding selection is beef with jade nan for $4.95. The meat is served with stir-fried pieces of fresh broccoli in a sweet sauce of sugar, soy, ginger and other ingredients. Ask your waiter for specific advice on ordering dishes which range from blindingly hot to fairly mild, including fresh seafood and several vegetarian choices.

HOUSE OF HUNAN, 3150 North Lincoln Avenue, Chicago. Telephone: 327-0427. Hours: 4 pm-10:30 pm, Monday-Thursday; until 11:30 pm Friday and Saturday; noon-10:30 pm, Sunday. Cards: AE, BA, DC, MC. Reservations accepted. Street parking can be difficult. Full bar service.

PORK

MOO SHU PORK (with four pan fried cakes). 4.50

HUNAN PORK 4.50

SHREDDED PORK with Peking Sauce 4.75

HUE-GOU PORK. 4.25

ROAST PORK with SEASONED VEGETABLES 4.75

PORK with GARLIC SAUCE 4.50

PORK with CHINESE PICKLE 4.75

SWEET & SOUR PORK 4.25

SWEET & SOUR SPARE RIBS 4.25

BEEF

BEEF with Mushrooms and Bamboo Shoots 4.95

MONGOLIAN BEEF 4.50

HUNAN BEEF. 5.20

BEEF SZECHUAN STYLE 4.95

BEEF with JADE NAN 4.95

WILLOW BEEF 4.95

BEEF with SNOW PEA PODS 4.95

BEEF with GREEN PEPPER 3.95

BEEF in OYSTER SAUCE 4.95

SHREDDED BEEF, Tea Sauce 4.75

SHREDDED BEEF HOME STYLE 5.25

SHREDDED BEEF, Peking Sauce 4.95

BEAN CURD with BEEF 3.95

Chicago
HUNGARIAN RESTAURANT
Hungarian

$

The atmosphere at Hungarian Restaurant has changed from the old days when it was like walking into a friend's kitchen where soup bubbled on the stove, meat simmered in the oven and the smell of rich seasonings hung in the air. Now there are Hungarian travel posters, a plastic grape trellis and red walls. But the food is as good as ever in this homey storefront restaurant with its 13 tables and a style sometimes less than polished. You won't spend a lot of money here and the Hungarian fare is splendid. The combination platter, as in other ethnic restaurants, is always a good choice for the novice. Of the entrées, the chicken paprikash is one of my favorites. The house salad is rather timid, but the desserts are excellent. Don't miss the palacsintas, the Hungarian version of French crêpes, wrapped around a filling of apricot preserves and sprinkled lightly on top with confectioners' sugar.

HUNGARIAN RESTAURANT, 4146 North Lincoln Avenue, Chicago. Telephone: 248-1003. Hours: 5 pm-10 pm, Monday and Wednesday-Saturday; noon-10 pm, Sunday; closed Tuesday. No cards. Reservations required on weekends only. Plentiful street parking. Full bar service; excellent selection of Hungarian wines.

Winnetka
THE INDIAN TRAIL
American $

This is home-style cooking at its finest—right in the heart of the wealthy North Shore. Ample portions are served by the same family which has run this culinary landmark for more than 40 years. Everything is fresh; I think they would even churn their own butter if they had the time and the staff. The menu changes daily and may range from steaks and chicken to duckling and trout. One caution: They are often busy and as they take no reservations, waits of up to an hour can be the rule, especially on weekends. But this place is worth it! The Indian Trail proves that in a world filled with change some things can remain the same.

THE INDIAN TRAIL, 807 Chestnut Street, Winnetka. Telephone: 446-1703. Hours: 11:30 am-2:30 pm; 4:30 pm-8 pm, Tuesday-Saturday; 11:30 am-7:30 pm, Sunday; closed Monday. Cards: BA, DC. Reservations not accepted. Street parking. No alcoholic beverages.

Northbrook
JAMES TAVERN
Early American

$$

A bicentennial gift to the Chicago area, James Tavern is a lovely recreation of an old Colonial inn. Replicas of period furniture are mixed with some genuine artifacts of early America to create the charming decor. The outstanding dinner-roll basket includes sticky sweet buns, cornbread sticks and old-fashioned Sally Lunn bread. Salads are mixed tableside in a sprightly herb dressing. Although owned and operated by Stouffer's, which is known for frozen prepackaged foods, everything is prepared from scratch in the James Tavern kitchen. I particularly like the veal birds and the crab cakes. The wine list is short but offers several outstanding selections; even Scuppernong, included perhaps more for authenticity than for taste, is among the potables.

JAMES TAVERN, Lake Cook Road (in the western quadrant of Northbrook Court Shopping Center), Northbrook. Telephone: 498-2020. Lunch: 11:30 am-3 pm, Monday-Saturday. Dinner: 5:30 pm-10 pm, Monday-Thursday; until 11 pm Friday and Saturday; 4:30 pm-8:30 pm, Sunday. Sunday brunch: 11:30 am-2:30 pm. Cards: AE, BA, DC, MC. Reservations suggested. Abundant free parking. Full bar service.

MAIN COURSE SELECTIONS

OLDE VIRGINIA CHICKEN FRICASSEE
Tender, succulent poultry pieces in a smooth, delicately-seasoned gravy served with a biscuit **3.95**

TRAVIS HOUSE ESCALLOPED OYSTERS
Oysters delectably baked in a ramekin with rich cream . . . **6.25**

SHENANDOAH FRONTIER GAME PYE
A hunter's treasure of venison, young fowl and rabbit with mushrooms in steaming gravy with a feather-light crust . . **6.95**

VEAL BIRDS
Delightful roulades of milk-fed veal cutlet. Filled with a most savory onion stuffing, then covered with an excellent Sherry Brown Sauce **8.50**

CAPTAIN'S CATCH OF BROILED FRESH FISH
The tantalizing flavour of only the freshest of fish, carefully broiled 'til golden brown, then laced with Lemon Butter . . . . **Market Price**

CHRISTIANA CAMPBELL'S MADE DISH OF SHRIMP & SCALLOPS
Mouthwatering bit-size morsels of shrimp and scallops. Combined expertly with fresh mushrooms, fine dry chablis wine and topped with Parmesan cheese crumbs . . . **7.50**

CASCADES FLOUNDER AMANDINE
The mild, pleasing taste of this fine fish is captured by sauteeing lightly in butter barely laced with lemon and lavished with almond bits **5.95**

TIDEWATER CRAB CAKES
Flaky crabmeat with a medley of pungent herbs, breaded and fried to a golden brown and served with tartar sauce **6.25**

BUCKINGHAM COUNTY PRIME RIB OF BEEF AU JUS WITH YORKSHIRE POPOVER **7.25**

KING'S PORTION PRIME RIB OF BEEF AU JUS WITH YORKSHIRE POPOVER
An extra generous portion designed to satisfy the expansive tastes of a monarch **8.50**

CHAR-BROILED FILET MIGNON **8.95**

STRIP STEAK WITH MUSHROOM CAPS **9.50**

OLDE FORGE BEEF BROCHETTE with Rice Pilaf   **6.95**

SEAFARER'S DOUBLET
Twin steamed Lobster Tails with drawn butter . . . **Market Price**

ALASKA KING CRAB LEGS **8.50**

Henry B. Clarke House

Chicago
JOVAN
French   **$$$**

The initial Chicago adventure of Jovan Trboyevic, this excellent French restaurant is back on the rise after a period of benign neglect when the proprietor's attentions were more taken up with Le Perroquet (which see). There is no printed menu. Fixed price dinners, recently at $13.50 per person, can change daily depending upon what is available from purveyors. You will find some items offered more regularly than others, such as an excellent gazpacho soup and delicately prepared brook trout in an herb and champagne sauce. Other fine choices are lamb chops in dill sauce, sliced tenderloin in port with truffles and roast duck in a complex apple-based sauce. Don't miss Grand Marnier soufflé for dessert. The wine list covers a broad spectrum from inexpensive Portuguese rosé all the way up to well-bred château vintages. Jovan displays the finesse which distinguishes the extraordinary from the merely good.

JOVAN FRENCH RESTAURANT, 16 East Huron, Chicago. Telephone: 944-7766. Lunch: noon-2 pm, Monday-Friday. Dinner: 6 pm-midnight, Monday-Saturday; closed Sunday. Cards: AE, DC. Reservations required. Valet parking. Full bar service.

Chicago
KAMEHACHI
Japanese

$$

There are many Japanese restaurants in Chicago, but this is the one visiting business executives from Tokyo run to for sushi, the popular snack of vinegared rice balls combined with fish or vegetables. If you are new to sushi, I suggest you tell them so at Kamahachi and let the sushi chef get you started on something easy like raw tuna in a semisweet soy sauce. Other sushi selections can include eel, octopus and squid. Entrées at Kamehachi represent some of the best Nipponese cuisine Chicago has to offer. The menu clearly explains what each dish is, from tempura and sukiyaki to kushi katsu. Service is pleasant; the restaurant is neat as the proverbial pin.

KAMEHACHI, 1617 North Wells, Chicago. Telephone: 664-3663. Lunch: noon-2:30 pm, Tuesday-Saturday. Dinner: 5 pm-11 pm, Tuesday-Thursday; until midnight Friday and Saturday; 5:30 pm-11 pm, Sunday. Cards: AE, BA. Reservations accepted. Street parking. Full bar service.

FROM OUR SUSHI BAR

SUSHI (A) .... 6 Sushi, 1 seaweed roll 5.00

SUSHI (B) DELUXE .... Assortment of fresh Seafood on vine-gared Rice cakes, 9 pieces 6.00

CHIRASHI .... Assortment of fresh Seafood on a bed of vinegared Rice 5.00

TEKKA DON .... Filet of fresh Tuna on a bed of vinegared rice 6.00

INARI ZUSHI .... 6 Bean cake pockets filled with rice 3.00

ENTREES LISTED BELOW INCLUDE RICE, SOUP, PICKLES, TEA

SASHIMI .... Filet of fresh Tuna 6.00

TEMPURA .... Shrimp and vegetable dipped in batter deep fried 5.00

TEMPURA (B) DELUXE .... Shrimp and vegetables - Larger portion 5.50

VEGETABLE TEMPURA .... Deep fried vegetables 4.00

KAKIAGE .... Tempura patty diced Shrimp, onions and green peppers fried 5.50

SUKIYAKI .... Tender Beef slices, green vegetables, Bean Cake, bamboo shoot and noodles 6.00

CHICKEN TERIYAKI .... Broiled Chicken. Teriyaki sauce 4.50

STEAK TERIYAKI .... Broiled Steak with Teriyaki sauce 6.00

BEEF KUSHIYAKI .... Beef, green pepper and onion on a skewer broiled with Teriyaki sauce. 5.50

KUSHI KATSU .... Deep fried, breaded Pork Tenderloin and onion on a skewer 5.50

TENDON .... Bowl of Rice topped with fried Shrimp and sauce 3.75

FRESH FISH .... Fried, broiled or Teriyaki 5.50

OCHA-ZUKE   Bowl of Rice with Tea

NORI CHA .... Seaweed 3.00

SHAKE CHA .... Salmon 3.50

TARAKO CHA .... Cod Roe 3.50

TEN CHA .... Fried Shrimp 3.50

MAGU CHA .... Filet of Tuna 4.00

Chicago
KHYBER
Indian $$

Khyber offers a wide variety of Indian foods. From tropical regions come highly seasoned curry dishes; from northern sections come the tandoori specialties, roasted in large clay urns over charcoal. I think combination dinners offer the best way to sample the range of possibilities. Begin with mulligatawny soup, a remnant from British Empire days. Then savor the different tastes and textures of several main courses: chicken tandoori, seikh kabab and lamb pasanda. The chicken has that wonderful charcoal flavor from the tandoor. The kabab is made from ground lamb rolled and skewered with onions. It, too, is roasted in the tandoor. Lamb pasanda is marinated in yogurt and served in a creamy sauce delicately spiced to perfection. Like most Indian restaurants, Khyber also features a wide selection of vegetarian selections. Desserts here are outstanding, particularly the sweet candies.

KHYBER INDIA RESTAURANT, 50 East Walton, Chicago. Telephone: 649-9060. Lunch: 11:30 am-2:30 pm, Monday-Saturday. Dinner: 5:30 pm-11:30 pm, Monday-Saturday. Closed Sunday. Cards: AE, BA, CB, DC, MC. Reservations suggested. Parking in Huguelet Garage (two-hour discount). Full bar service.

TANDOOR
CLAY OVEN PREPARATIONS

TANDOORI MURGH   half   2.75
Chicken marinated in yogurt and spices, cooked on charcoal in   full   5.25
clay ovens

MURGH TIKKA   3.75
Boneless chicken pieces cooked in clay oven

BOTI KABAB   3.75
Cubed leg of lamb roasted in clay oven

SEIKH KABAB   3.75
Minced lamb mixed with onions, herbs, spices, hand rolled on skew
cooked in clay ovens

TANDOORI MACHHLI   5.50
Whole trout or pike mildly spiced and baked in clay oven

MACHHLI TIKKA   3.75
Boneless fish pieces roasted in clay oven

TANDOORI MIXED GRILL   5.50
An assortment of Tandoori Chicken, and various other Tikkas and Kababs

LAZIZ MACHHLI
SEAFOOD DELICACIES

JHINGA BHUNA   3.95
Succulent shrimps cooked in flavorful gravy

JHINGA MASALA   3.95
Shrimps cooked with green peppers, onions and tomatoes

MACHHLI CURRY   3.95
Boneless fish cooked in mildly spiced gravy

BIRYANI AND PULLAO
RICE SPECIALITIES

PLAIN RICE   .75

MATTAR PULLAO   1.50

NAVRATTAN PULLAO   2.25
Rice cooked with a touch of saffron and garden fresh vegetables

GOSHT BIRYANI   3.50
Saffron rice cooked with tender lamb

SHAHJAHANI BIRYANI   3.50
Saffron rice cooked with boneless chicken, garnished with boiled eggs,
herbs and nuts

Chicago
LA BOUILLABAISSE
French

$$

Build a better restaurant in Chicago and the city will beat a path to your door, wherever it is. It is not uncommon for restaurants of taste and graciousness to open in shabby or industrial neighborhoods. With that in mind, ignore the commercial activity outside and enjoy the food inside La Bouillabaisse. Naturally the specialty is their namesake, the marvelous fish stew probably not made alike in any two places in the world. The most expensive selection on the menu at $11.75, it is as tasteful and hearty a bowlful as you are likely to find anywhere. Other entrées are less costly—in the $6 to $8 range—and all include bread, salad, and vegetables plus rice or potatoes. The emphasis is on the provincial school of French cooking. From time to time preparations of rabbit, venison, pheasant or other game are offered. I like the freshness and style of La Bouillabaisse. Their sign is poorly lit so you may have to look closely to find the restaurant.

LA BOUILLABAISSE, 1418 West Fullerton, Chicago. Telephone: 549-9197 or 281-5688. Hours: 11 am-11 pm, Tuesday-Friday; 6 pm-11 pm, Saturday and Sunday; closed Monday. Cards: MC. Reservations suggested weeknights, required on weekends. Street parking. Full bar service.

PLAT DU JOUR

ask your waiter or waitress

FILET OF SOLE   5 50
baked in wine demon and tomatoes

CRABE (LEGS)   7 50
with Garlic Butter and parsil

LANGOUSTE (lobster) 9 25
with butter

LANGOUSTE   10 50
harmoricaine sauce

STEAK au poivre   6 50
STEAK madere sauce   7 50
FILET MIGNON   8 50

DAUBE   5 50
beef stew in wine sauce

ALLOUETTE   6 75
rolled steak with mushroons ham
and wine sauce

CANARD a d'orange
8 50

COQ au VIN   5 50

Chicago
LA CHEMINÉE
French

$$$

One of the most romantic spots in town, La Cheminée is all brick walls, low ceilings and French country ambience. The restaurant oozes coziness, although on busy evenings, closely packed tables can detract from that special intimacy. The fixed price dinner is $13.50, although some selections will raise that cost. La Cheminée offers a wide selection of consistently well-prepared French food. Sauces are flavorful and portions hearty, whether you choose a simple tournedo with béarnaise or a complex duckling in green peppercorn sauce. Desserts are luscious and, where required, abundantly creamy as in the peach or strawberry melba. The wine list is quite extensive and includes several Grand Cru selections.

LA CHEMINÉE, 1161 North Dearborn, Chicago. Telephone: 642-6654. Lunch: 11:30 am-2:30 pm, Monday-Friday. Dinner: 5:30 pm-11 pm, Monday-Saturday. Closed Sunday. Cards: AE, BA, CB, DC, MC. Reservations required. Parking at public garage one block west on Elm Street (at discount). Full bar service.

Poissons

Cuisses de Grenouilles Provençale (Frog Legs Sauté)
Petits Crabes aux Raisins (Soft Shell Crabs with Grapes)
Turbot Poché Hollandaise or Sauté Béarnaise   1.00
Sole Amandine (Dover Sole with Almonds)
Homard à L' Americaine (Lobster in Brandy Sauce) 2.00
Truite Farcie (Trout Stuffed with Seafood Mousse)

Volaille

Coq au Vin (Chicken in Red Wine Sauce)
Canard à l' Orange (Roast Duckling in Orange Sauce)

Viande

Steak au Poivre (French Pepper Steak)
Veau Piccata (Veal Sauted in Marsala Wine)
Veau Florentine (Veal with Spinach in Cream Sauce, Gratinée)
Foie de Veau Sauté (Calf Liver Sauté with Bacon)
Côtes d' Agneau (Broiled Lamb Chops)
Entrecôte Grillée (Broiled Sirloin Steak)
La Brochette de Filet Maison
(Broiled on Skewer, Peppers, Mushrooms, Tomato)
Tournedo Béarnaise (Beef Tenderloin with Béarnaise Sauce)   1.00
Chateaubriand Béarnaise (For 2 - 3.00)
Cervelle de Veau (Calf Brains Sauté with Capers)
Beef Wellington (Tenderloin in Pastry Crust)
Carré d' Agneau (Rack of Lamb)   1.75
(Not Responsible for Meat Ordered Well Done)

Chicago
LA CHOZA
Mexican

$

In a down-at-the-heels neighborhood, La Choza is yet another proof of that Chicago axiom: Location means little to a restaurant's success. La Choza just happens to be "the" Mexican restaurant for taco and tortilla buffs. This place is so authentic I am almost tempted to bring my own water. Fortunately, the water's fine, so eat with gusto, but be prepared for some spicy seasonings. For appetizers, Mexican pizzas called kamoosh are real favorites; the garlic soup is also a winner, and guaranteed to keep away vampires. Mole de pollo with its bittersweet chocolate aftertaste, is a good choice among the main courses. Among the desserts, the flan for 75 cents is numero uno.

LA CHOZA, 7630 North Paulina, Chicago. Telephone: 761-8020 or 465-9401. Hours: noon-11:30 pm, Tuesday-Friday; until midnight Saturday; until 10:30 pm Sunday; closed Monday. No cards. No reservations. Parking in lot across the street. Full bar service.

Arlington Heights
LA POÊLE D'OR
Omelettes/Crêpes

$

Whether you call them blintzes, palacsintas or crêpes, they all fall in the same category of a thin pancake stuffed with filling. The French have elevated crêpe making into a mini-art. La Poêle d'Or serves crêpes and omelettes that are not only culinary delights, but the portions are so large you'll be hard-pressed to clean your plate. Top-of-the-line crêpes are the cardinale and the imperiale; both depend upon an excellent lobster cream sauce for their success. For beef eaters, the ambassadeur is reminiscent of a stuffed green pepper in its texture and pungency. The Basque crêpe is another example of the crêpe maker's art at its apogee. The seven omelettes on the menu include a delicious omelette chasseur with the traditional hunter's sauce. If you can still handle dessert after the Brobdingnagian portions, order a slice of the house cheesecake. A hint of Grand Marnier marries well with the blend of cream cheese and whipping cream frozen in a thin sweet crust.

LE POÊLE D'OR, 1121 South Arlington Heights Road, Arlington Heights. Telephone: 593-9148. Hours: 11:30 am-8:30 pm, Sunday and Tuesday-Thursday; until 10 pm Friday and Saturday; closed Monday. No cards. No reservations. Free parking in shopping center lot. No alcoholic beverages; you may bring your own wine.

Chicago
LA FONTAINE
French

$$$

This pleasant country French atmosphere of brick, flowered wallpapers, and fireplaces is a lovely setting for the enjoyment of satisfying French cuisine. Located on a busy stretch of North Clark Street, La Fontaine nevertheless manages to exclude all that, wrapping diners up into its own little world. The $13.50 fixed price dinner includes appetizer or soup, salad, main course, dessert and coffee or tea. The French onion soup gratinée is bountiful; vichyssoise is appropriately delicate. Among main course selections, the salmon "grand nord" is unique. Paper-thin slices of fish protect a stuffing of crab meat and mushrooms and are served decoratively with champagne and lobster sauces. The beef Wellington works as well as this meat lover's specialty ever can; the portion is ample, not overpowered by too much pastry. Veal Normande is another of the splendid main course selections. Salad in a tarragon-accented dressing is most refreshing after the entrée. Desserts vary from time to time, but usually include a fruit tart, profiteroles and chocolate mousse. The wine selection is commensurate with the level of the cuisine; medium-priced house recommendations can help cut the shock of a large dinner check.

LA FONTAINE, 2442 North Clark Street, Chicago. Telephone: 525-1800. Lunch: 11:30 am-2:30 pm, Tuesday-Friday. Dinner: 5:30 pm-10:30 pm, Monday-Thursday; until 11 pm Friday and Saturday; closed Sunday. Cards: AE, BA, DC, MC. Reservations required. Parking in Texaco garage across the street (at discount). Full bar service.

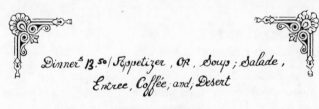

Dinner 13.50 / Appetizer, OR, Soups; Salade,
Entree, Coffée, and, Desert

✻✻Nos Specialites✻✻

~Le Filet de Boeuf en Croute ~ Sauce Girolles
    (beef wellington with special mushroom sauce)
~La Truite Soufflée "Jean de La Fontaine"
    (trout soufflée champagne sauce)
~Le Veau Saute Normande
    (veal sauted with applejack, mushrooms, cream sauce)
~Le Supreme de Volaille "Belle France"
    (breast of chicken with ham and cheese)
~La Paupiette de Saumon "Grand Nord"
    (salmon stuffed with crab meat and fresh mushrooms)
~Le Filet de Lotte
    (filet of white monk fish
~La Cocotte de Boeuf "a Livrogne"
    (beef, fresh mushrooms and onions, red wine sauce)
~Le Canard Roti Façon du Chef (2 personnes)
    (roast duck with peaches and orange sauce)

✻✻Nos Grillades✻✻ ($1.25 sup)

~Le Coeur de Charolais Grille Sauce Bearnaise
    (filet mignon ~ sauce bearnaise)
~L'Entrecote Poellee aux Echalottes
    (sirloin sauted with shallots)
~L'Entrecote Grillee Bearnaise
    (sirloin ~ sauce bearnaise)
~La Cote D'agneau "Bouquet de Provence"
    (lamb chops marinated in herbs and broiled)

✻✻Nos Poissons✻✻ ($1.25 sup)

~La Sole de Douvre "Meunière"
    (dover sole in butter, lemon sauce)
~Le Filet de Turbot Poché "Sauce Hollandaise"
    (poached turbot ~ hollandaise sauce)

Chicago
LA FONTANELLA
Northern Italian

$$

The likelihood is that most people's idea of what Italian food should be has been primarily influenced by exposure to Sicilian and Neapolitan restaurants. In fact, an entirely different style of cooking dominates most of Italy north of Rome. The cuisine is Tuscan, where sauces are gentler and seasonings more delicate. La Fontanella has a largely Tuscan menu although some specialties, such as fried meat and rice balls (called arancini), are more commonly found in kitchens to the south. In this cozy and somewhat romantic restaurant complete dinners include everything from soup or salad to dessert and coffee. Among main course highlights is lamb scaloppini with hearts of artichoke. The mild sauce, lightly enhanced with tomatoes, does not obscure the delicacy of the lamb. Among four chicken dishes, chicken alla Franca is a family recipe. For dessert try cannoli, the sweet crusty pastry tubes filled with creamed sweet cheese that practically ooze deliciousness.

LA FONTANELLA, 2414 South Oakley Boulevard, Chicago. Telephone: 927-5249. Hours: 11 am-midnight, Tuesday-Friday; 4:30 pm-midnight, Saturday and Sunday; closed Monday. No cards. Reservations required. Street parking. Full bar service.

Pasta

Served with Meat Sauce or Tomato Sauce

Served with Meat Balls or Sausage .... .75 extra

SPAGHETTI	2.00		GNOCCHI	2.50
MOSTACCIOLI	2.00		RAVIOLI	2.75
SPAGHETTI ALL'OLIO	2.00		TORTELLINI	2.50
PASTA VERDE			LASAGNA	2.50
in Cream Sauce	2.50		MANICOTTI	2.75

Favorite Meat Specialties

	DINNER	A LA CARTE
VEAL SCALOPPINI	5.50	4.00
(thin slices of veal sauteed in wine with mushrooms)		
SALTIMBOCCA ALLA ROMANA	5.75	4.25
(veal sauteed in wine with herbs and prosciutto)		
VEAL PARMIGIANA	5.75	4.25
(veal cutlet with tomato sauce, mushrooms, and melted cheese)		
LAMB SCALOPPINI	5.50	4.00
(lamb sauteed in wine with artichoke hearts)		
CHICKEN CACCIATORE	5.00	3.50
(chicken stewed in tomato sauce, mushrooms, and olives)		
CHICKEN ALLA FRANCA	5.00	3.50
(chicken stuffed with garlic butter, lightly breaded, fried, then baked)		
CHICKEN VESUVIO	5.00	3.50
(chicken lightly browned and baked with garlic, olive oil, herbs, and a hint of lemon)		
CHICKEN, FRIED OR BROILED	5.00	3.50

Steaks • Chops • Cutlets

	DINNER	A LA CARTE		DINNER	A LA CARTE
T-BONE	8.50	7.00	BROILED LAMB CHOPS	5.50	4.00
FILET	8.00	6.50	BROILED PORK CHOPS	5.50	4.00
VEAL CUTLET	5.50	4.00			

Sea Food

FRIED SHRIMP	5.50	4.00	FRIED CALAMARI	5.00	3.50
PERCH			CALAMARI ROMANA		
Breaded or Broiled	5.00	3.50	with Linguini	5.00	3.50
	SCAMPI	6.00	4.50		
	in Garlic Butter Sauce				

DINNER includes choice of soup or mostaccioli, salad, dessert & coffee

Chicago
LA LLAMA
Peruvian

$$$

This is the newest of three Peruvian restaurants operated by members of the Asturrizaga family. As at the other two, El Inca and Piqueo, there is no printed menu at La Llama. Dinners are fixed price at $10 and include appetizers, soup, main course, vegetables, dessert, coffee and maybe even an extra surprise or two. Among excellent appetizers is turbot fried and served in a wine-based marinade with a hint of chili pepper amidst its complex seasonings. Finely chopped broccoli molded into patties, battered and deep fried is served in a creamy sauce not without some spiciness. Other taste treats are a soufflé of puréed artichokes and asparagus, and potatoes stuffed with ground beef, raisins and seasonings and fried until crusty and golden. A popular main course among several rotated regularly is charcoal-broiled beef on skewers, served with a hot red sauce. For dessert we favor the strawberry flan, as light and creamy as can be. Excellent Peruvian coffee tops off one of the best meals served in the Chicago area regardless of price.

LA LLAMA, 2651 West Peterson, Chicago. Telephone: 784-9757. Hours: 5 pm-10 pm, daily. Cards: AE, CB, DC. Reservations suggested on weekends. Street parking. No bar service; you may bring your own wine.

Chicago
LAWRENCE OF OREGANO
Italian

$$

A sense of humor helps a restaurant; good food helps more. This place has both. It is one of the Lettuce Entertain You, Inc. group (see Great Gritzbe's and R.J. Grunts) and may be the best. Genuinely good Italian food includes great braccioli (a rolled and stuffed steak), excellent tomato sauce and pastas prepared just right. Vegetable presentation is quite good, particularly the fried zucchini—not on the menu, but brought as a complimentary serving by your waiter or waitress. Waiters and waitresses, incidentally, are all performers who get up and strut their stuff in the front restaurant cafe section. Lawrence of Oregano also features a carry-out Italian delicatessen where you can purchase sausages, cheeses and other goodies. Mange!

LAWRENCE OF OREGANO, 662 West Diversey Parkway, Chicago. Telephone: 871-1916. Hours: 11:30 am-midnight, Monday-Thursday; until 1 am Friday and Saturday; 4 pm-midnight, Sunday. No cards. Reservations accepted. Parking at nearby garage (at discount). Full bar service.

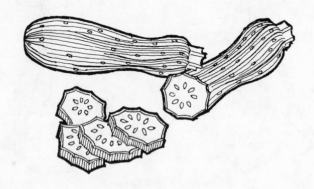

Chicago
LAWRY'S
American (Prime Rib)

$$

An import from Los Angeles (yes, they are the same people who make the seasoned salt) this is the place to go for prime rib in Chicago. Lawry's is located in an old mansion which once housed the fabled Kungsholm Restaurant, but a million-dollar renovation has created an entirely new setting. The only entrée served is roast beef. It comes in three cuts: English (sliced thinly) for $8.95, Lawry for $8.95 and the large Chicago cut for $10.75. Full standing rib roasts are prepared in a bank of eight electric ovens over a bed of rock salt and seasonings. Then each roast is put on a temperature-controlled silver serving cart for individual carving at tableside. Dinners include salad; baked potato and vegetables are à la carte as are sweet desserts—nearly as grandiose as the cuts of beef. Good California house wines are available or you may order from an extensive list. The luncheon menu is more varied.

LAWRY'S THE PRIME RIB, 100 East Ontario, Chicago. Telephone: 787-5000. Lunch: 11:30 am-2 pm, Monday-Friday; sandwich bar until 2:30 pm. Dinner: 5 pm-11 pm, Monday-Friday; until midnight Saturday; 3 pm-10 pm, Sunday. Cards: AE, BA, DC, MC. Reservations required. Valet parking ($2). Full bar service.

Chicago
LE BASTILLE
French

$$$

Le Bastille is not a prison, but a lovely little restaurant which offers up a periodically changing selection of table d'hôte lunches and dinners in two different dining rooms. One room has the charm of floral prints in a country setting; the other, which is my favorite, provides a more rustic provincial style with a beamed ceiling, fireplace (artificial, sad to say), patterned wallpapers and decorative crockery. A fairly new chef seems to have a light touch with sauces, allowing them to accent rather than dominate their respective dishes. Recommended entrées include lobster thermidor, veal Normande and any of the seafood preparations. The menu changes periodically. Le Bastille's proprietor, René Martin, is as jolly a Frenchman to come down the pike since Lucky Pierre. He is a marvelous host.

LE BASTILLE, 21 West Superior, Chicago. Telephone: 787-2050. Lunch: 11:30 am-2:30 pm, Monday-Friday. Dinner: 5:30 pm-10:30 pm, Monday-Friday; until 11 pm Saturday; closed Sunday. Cards: AE, BA, CB, DC, MC. Reservations required. Free valet parking. Full bar service.

DINNER

*Price includes entree, vegetables,
house salade and coffee*

HORS D'OEUVRES

Escargots 3.50   Hearts of Palm Vinaigrette 2.50

Shrimp Cocktail 2.75

Baked Oysters 2.95   Ratatouille 2.75

Clams or Blue Points 2.75 Smoked Salmon 2.75

Smoked Ham 2.75 Champignons à la Greeque 1.95

POTAGES

Onion Soup 1.95   Vichyssoise 1.50 Soup of the Day 1.50

ENTREES

Fresh Lobster Thermidor or Steamed Lobster 11.95

Dover Sole Meuniere or Amandine 11.95

Bouillabaisse Riviera (20 minutes) 11.95

Veal Normande or Saute Citron 11.95

Baby Calf Liver 11.95

Steak au Poivre 11.95

Sirloin Steak Maitre d'Hotel 11.95

Filet Mignon Bearnaise 11.95

FOR TWO

Rack of Lamb Persillé 26.95

Chateaubriand Sauce Bearnaise 26.95

Potatoes and Vegetables of the Day

SALADES

Watercress 2.00   Tomato 1.50   Avocado Salade 2.00

Bastille Salade 2.25   House Salade 1.50

DESSERTS

Mousse au Chocolat or Creme Caramel 1.75

Ice Cream or Sherbet 1.50

Strawberries in Red Wine 1.50

Cheeses 1.95   Crepes Suzettes 3.50 (for two)

Chicago
LEE'S CANTON CAFE
Chinese (Cantonese)

$$

In the rush of some diners to explore the subtleties of the now fashionable cuisines of Szechwan and Northern China, the old standby, Cantonese, may be ignored. And that is a shame, because in the hands of artists, good Cantonese food can be unusual and delicious. Some evening, forget your neighborhood carry-out, put a group of eight or 10 people together and visit Lee's Canton Cafe. Here is a menu that is more than chow mein, chop suey and fried rice. For appetizers try crab Rangoon, a fried won ton noodle stuffed with crab meat—not to be missed. Sui mi are dumplings filled with fried meat and chicken. Shrimp toast, a spread of minced shrimp on a thick crustless dough, is deep fried and sprinkled with sesame seeds. Outstanding main course selections include incredibly delicious sweet and sour softshelled crab. Beef eaters should try the Tony special; similar to Hong Kong steak, the beef slices come in an oyster sauce with mushrooms and snow peas. Portions are large and the food is in a class by itself. This is one of the better restaurants in Chinatown and is a real favorite with those who know.

LEE'S CANTON CAFE, 2300 South Wentworth Avenue, Chicago. Telephone: 225-4838 or 225-4861. Hours: 11 am-11:30 pm, Sunday-Thursday; until 12:30 am Friday and Saturday. Cards: AE. Reservations accepted. Street parking or community lot. Full bar service.

CANTONESE DISHES

BEEF — CANTONESE STYLE

BITTER MELON WITH BEEF......................2.95
BEEF (with Oyster Sauce)........................3.75
CURRY BEEF...................................3.75
BEEF KEW (Beef with Chinese Vegetables)........3.50
STEAK KEW (Sirloin with Chinese Vegetables).....5.95
BEEF WITH STRING BEANS (Chopped or Regular).. 2.75
SUT DOWL MAR TA GNOW (Beef with Snow Peas
   and Water Chestnuts)...........................3.95
PEPPER BEEF WITH OR WITHOUT TOMATO......2.75
BEEF BOCK CHOY (Beef with Chinese Greens).....2.75
BEEF ALMOND DEN..............................3.95
SNOW PEAS WITH BEEF..........................3.50
HONG KONG STEAK.............................7.95
TONY SPECIAL (One of our customer's famous dishes
   Tender Steak with Mushrooms, Pea Pods
   and Cooked with Oyster Sauce)...................7.95

SEAFOOD — CANTONESE STYLE

STEAMED WHITE FISH...........................3.25
SWEET AND SOUR SOFT SHELL CRAB...........5.25
CHOW LONE HARR (Jumbo Live Lobster with Shell
   Cantonese Style.........................7.50 and up
CHOW LONE HARR KEW
   (Lobster Meat with Vegetables).................6.15
CHOW HARR KEW
   (Fresh Shrimp with Chinese Vegetables)........4.35
HONG SUI HARR
   (Shrimp Fritters with Chinese Vegetables)......4.35
FRESH SHRIMP ALMOND DEN 4.35
FRESH LOBSTER ALMOND DEN..................6.15
SWEET AND SOUR SHRIMP......................4.35
FRESH SHRIMP WITH LOBSTER SAUCE
   or GARLIC SAUCE............................3.95
STEAMED YELLOW PIKE...................5.00 and up
SLICED FISH (with Mixed Chinese Vegetables).....4.15
FRIED LOBSTER WITHOUT SHELL OR
WITH SHELL (Cantonese Style) 8.95
SNAIL CHINESE STYLE..........................2.95
VERMERCELLI WITH SHRIMP....................3.75

Chicago
LE FESTIVAL
French

$$$

One of Chicago's newer French restaurants, Le Festival is on the way to resounding success. Small and intimate, Le Festival occupies a renovated town house which has been home to at least two other restaurants. Dinners are served for no more than 70 people at any one time. Floors are overlaid with Oriental rugs, tapestries adorn the walls and lighting is soft. The fixed price dinner ($13.50) includes choice of appetizer or soup, salad, entrée, dessert and coffee or tea. Among the appetizers try the pheasant pâté, a coarse grind of meat bound with cognac and port wine. Onion soup is topped with a copious amount of cheese thickly covering the top of the baking crock. From the entrées outstanding preparations include veal Normande and lobster thermidor. Service is excellent; the wine list has moderate depth.

LE FESTIVAL, 28 West Elm Street, Chicago. Telephone: 944-7090. Lunch: 11:30 am-2:30 pm, Monday-Friday. Dinner: 5:30 pm-10:30 pm, Monday-Friday; until 11 pm Saturday; closed Sunday. Cards: AE, BA, MC. Reservations required. Street parking; nearby public lot. Full bar service.

Entrees

Rognos De Veau Dijonnaise
veal kidneys in mustard sauce

Veau Florentine
veal, spinach, cream sauce, gratinee

Steak Au Poivre
sirloin steak, ground pepper, cognac, flamed

Tournedos Rossini
beef tenderloin, goose liver, truffles and wine sauce

Coq Au Chambertin
chicken, bacon, mushrooms, onions, red wine sauce

Médaillon De Veau Normande
veal, apple jack, mushrooms, cream

Boeuf Stroganoff

Tournedos Bearnaise

Canard A L'Orange
roast duck, orange sauce

For Two
+
two dollars per person

Chateaubriand Bearnaise

Carré D'Agneau Bouquetière

Faisan Souvaroff
roast pheasant, goose liver, truffles, port wine sauce

Wheeling
LE FRANÇAIS
French

$$$

Le Français is not to be described; it is to be experienced. This one restaurant has put the small town of Wheeling on the gourmet map of America. Chef Jean Banchet is an ardent student of Brillat-Savarin, Auguste Escoffier and Paul Bocuse. As a result, dazzling carts and trays of foods, from pâtés to pastries, are paraded here before the eyes of gaping diners who ordinarily would not see such artistry outside of gourmet society dinners. Among chef Banchet's proudest accomplishments are his deft preparations of pâtés and terrines, his fish en croûte à la Paul Bocuse, and his mastery of sauces. The fish à la Bocuse may be salmon, turbot or sea bass depending on what is available. The fish is topped with a lobster mousse, baked in a pastry which has been sculpted down to the last gill and fin to resemble the fish it encloses. This creation is served with two, and sometimes three, sauces. You won't find this dish on the printed menu, but it probably will be among the 10 or 12 specialty items offered each night. If fine food is holy, Le Français is its temple and Jean Banchet the high priest.

LE FRANÇAIS, 269 South Milwaukee, Wheeling. Telephone: 541-7470. Hours: 5:30 pm-9:30 pm, Tuesday-Sunday; closed Monday. Cards: AE, BA, MC. Reservations required. Free valet parking. Full bar service.

LES PLATS DU PATRON

La dodine de Caneton au Vinaigre - 12.50
(Stuffed Breast of Duck with Vinegar Sauce)

Le Pigeon Farci Poelé aux Gousses d'ail - 12.50
(Roast Squab with Garlic Cloves)

La Noix de Ris de Veau des Deux Siecles - 14.50
(Fresh Sweet Bread Bicentennial)

La Jambonnette de Faisan aux Morilles - 14.50
(Stuffed Breast of Pheasant with Morrel Mushrooms and Cream Sauce)

La Cote de Veau aux Petits Legumes - 13.50
(Veal Chop Saute with Fresh Vegetables)

Le Carré d'Agneau Persillé aux Salsifis - 30.00
(Lamb Rack for 2 with Salsifis and Herbs)

L'entrecote Geante Pour deux a la Moelle et aux Cepes - 30.00
(Double Sirloin for Two with Shallots, Red Wine, Marrow, Wild Mushrooms)

La Poularde Sautée à L'estragon - 11.50
(Fresh Capon Saute' with Fresh Tarragon White Wine Cream Sauce)

Chicago
LE PERROQUET
French

$$$

Le Perroquet is the finest jewel in Chicago's restaurant crown. The fixed price of $21.50 per person is worth every penny. The restaurant is distinguished from others by a pastel ambience of cheerful sophistication and a certain élan that exists among the staff. The "nouvelle cuisine" is ably demonstrated here. After you have been seated, a waiter will bring a platter of canapes to your table, little tidbits to enjoy with kir or cocktail. Appetizers may include smoked salmon, melon in port wine, perhaps a salmon mousse in green pepper sauce. A highlight of exquisite delicacy is the mushroom pastry tart with cream sauce. Among soups, the lobster bisque and the gazpacho remain my favorites. For the main course there are three or four daily specials not on the menu. Often, rack of veal is served; sea bass and turbot are popular fish presentations. Sauces, whether dark or light, are perfect down to the final stroke of the saucier's whisk. Dessert selections always include outstanding chocolate mousse, pastries and Grand Marnier soufflé. After-dinner mints hold sweet chocolate inside a dusting of bittersweet chocolate powder, the final touch to an always perfect meal.

LE PERROQUET, 70 East Walton, Chicago. Telephone: 944-7990. Lunch: noon-3 pm, Monday-Friday ($9.50 prix fixe). Dinner: 6 pm-10 pm, Monday-Saturday. Closed Sunday. Cards: AE, DC, house accounts. Reservations required. Men must wear coat and tie. Parking in nearby lots or garages. Full bar service; excellent wine list.

LES SURPRISES
BLUE POINTS
POTAGE DU JOUR
PÂTÉS ASSORTIS
MOUSSE DE SAUMON
BISQUE DE HOMARD
SAUMON FUMÉ (IMPORTÉ)
CAVIAR MALOSSOL DE BELUGA (16.00)
LA TRUFFE EN FEUILLETAGE (6.00)
LES ESCARGOTS
TOURTE AUX CHAMPIGNONS
CONSOMMÉ À L'ESSENCE DE TRUFFE

LES POISSONS FRAIS
ESCALOPES DE VEAU GRILLÉ
RIS DE VEAU AU BEURRE D'ESTRAGON
NOS PLATS DU JOUR
CANETON RÔTI MAISON (2 PERS.)
DODINE DE PIGEON
CONFIT D'OIE, POMMES SARLADAISE
SELLE D'AGNEAU À L'ORIENTALE
CARRÉ D'AGNEAU PÔELÉ
TOURNEDOS AUX ECHALOTES
STEAK À LA DIJONNAISE
PIÈCE DE BOEUF, SAUCE ENCHOITÉE

Chicago
L'ÉPUISETTE
French   **$$**

L'Épuisette is a little jewel box of a restaurant which continues year after year to present fine food in a fine atmosphere. Dim lighting and muraled walls of 18th century harbor fishing scenes set the ambience. Begin with soup, such as an always fine red snapper with a good deal of the snap still in it. Trout meunière stuffed with crab meat is a house specialty. When in season, soft shell crabs are a real delicacy, sautéed in butter and served with slivers of golden almond for a texture accent. Complete your dinner with coffee and dessert, perhaps a coconut snowball or cheesecake. A more than adequate wine list and service that fits the standard of the food have helped make L'Épuisette a favorite with knowledgeable Chicagoans and their guests.

L'ÉPUISETTE, 21 West Goethe, Chicago. Telephone: 944-2288. Hours: 5 pm-11 pm, Tuesday-Sunday, closed Monday. Cards: AE, BA, CB, DC, MC. Reservations required. Parking in building garage or nearby lots. Full bar service.

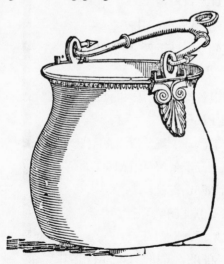

table d'hote dinners

APPETIZERS

Shrimp Cocktail Maison   .95
Half Grapefruit
Red Snapper Soup
Baked Crabmeat in shell (4)   1.60
Avocado Pear with Crabmeat   1.50
Filets of Marinated Herring   .95
Imported Sardines a la Francaise

Boston Clam Chowder
Lump Crabmeat Cocktail   2.50
Fruite Cocktail Marasquin
Melon in Season
Smoked Salmon   1.50
Tomato or V-8 Juice Cocktail
Blue Points or Cherrystones   1.25

L'EPUISETTE'S CHEF'S SPECIALS

Rocky Mountain Brook Trout, Meunière
(Boneless, Stuffed with Crabmeat) **9.95**

Filet of Dover Sole Marguery
(Truly a French Creation) **11.50**

Baked Shrimp de Jonghe
A Touch of Wine and Garlic makes it a delicious dish **9.95**

Lake Superior Whitefish, Maître d'Hotel, Broiled with Lemon Butter 9.25

Crepes l'Epuisette, Fresh Crabmeat Wrapped in Pancake, Sauce Mornay 9.75

Tenderloin Tips French Market, Served with Noodles 8.95

Crabmeat au Vin Blanc, Sauté with Shallots and Mushrooms 9.75

Fresh Shrimps Newburg or a la Creole, Very Tasty Dishes 9.50

Fresh Soft Shell Crabs Saute, Almond Butter (in season) 9.15

Stuffed Baked Deviled Crab 9.45

Scampi Buongusto, Shrimps Broiled in Garlic Butter, White Rice 9.50

Lobster Tails and Steak Duet 11.50

Choice of Potato or Vegetable du Jour and
Caesar, Mixed Green, Steak Tomato or Tomatoes with Sliced Onions and Cucumber Salad
Garlic, Clear French or Thousand Island Dressing

Creamy Roquefort Cheese   .50 additional

LES DESSERTS

Cheese Cake   Fromage   Profiterole   Snowball

Lime or Orange Sherbet   Fruit Compote   Half Grapefruit

Mocha Rum Cake   Melon in Season   Choice of Sundae or Parfait

Ice Creams: Vanilla, Coffee, Rum or Butter Pecan

BEVERAGE

Coffee   Tea

Chicago
L'ESCARGOT
French

$$$

Here in a decidedly non-Gallic neighborhood is the kind of charm that can sweep you into the arms of France. The restaurant is divided into two sections. A conventionally decorated dining room is to the right of the foyer; a long bar with booths and church pew-like banquettes is opposite. Chef Lucien Verge's beautifully prepared dishes seem to have a character unlike that found in other French restaurants in Chicago. The slant is definitely to the countryside rather than to the sophistication of Parisian cuisine. Any of the cassoulets are recommended; veal dishes are also handled nicely. Dinner prices include appetizer, soup, entrée, salad, dessert and coffee. House wines are solid upstanding selections available by glass or carafe. Bottled wines are listed by vintage. With the cozy atmosphere and true Gallic flair of L'Escargot, I wouldn't be surprised to find a couple of British or American airmen hiding in the cellar awaiting transfer by the Résistance back to England. Vive la France; vive L'Escargot.

L'ESCARGOT FRENCH RESTAURANT, 2925 North Halsted, Chicago. Telephone: 525-5525. Hours: 5 pm-9:30 pm, Monday-Thursday; until 10:30 pm Friday and Saturday; closed Sunday. Cards: AE, BA, DC, MC. Reservations required. Street parking. Full bar service.

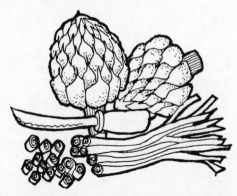

Les Hors d'Oeuvre (one choice included with dinner)

Le Canapé d'Anchois. (Anchovies on sliced tomatoes, vinaigrette sauce)

Smoked Filet of Herring with vinegar.

Les clams ravigote.

Maquereau au Vin blanc. (Mackerel in wine sauce)

Tomate Antiboise (Tomato stuffed with vegetable salade and mayonnaise)

Céleri remoulade (Julienne of celery root with mustard and mayonnaise)

Champignons à la Grecque (Btd mushrooms in wine and herbs sauce)

Oeuf dur Andalouse (Hard boiled egg on toast, sweet peppers, tomato and mayonnaise sauce)

Feuilleteaux oignons (Pastry shell filled with onions)

Paté de campagne   Melon de Saison

+ .50   Artichaut vinaigrette (fresh artichoke in vinaigrette sauce)

+ 1.00   Caviar Rouge (red caviar with sour cream)

+ 1.00   Saucisson Chaud en Croûte (Home made sausage baked in pastry crust)

+ 2.00   Avocat aux crevettes (Avocado and Shrimps mayonnaise)

+ 2.50   Escargots de Bourgogne (6 Snails in Shells, baked with garlic butter)

Les Entrées

Endives Flamande   9.50
(Belgian endives wrapped in ham, baked with cream sauce and Swiss cheese)

Curry d'Agneau à l'Indienne   9.50
(Lamb curry with chutney)

Sole Caprice   13.50
(Dover Sole sautéed in butter with lemon and Banana)

Truite Paiva   11.50
(Fresh Brook Trout, stuffed with mushroom purée, lobster sauce)

Cervelle meunière aux capres   10.50
(Fresh calf brain sauteed in butter and capers)

Poulet rôti sauce champagne   10.50
(Roast chicken with mushrooms and small onions, champagne sauce)

Canard rôti à l'orange   12.50
(Boneless duckling with orange sauce and wild rice)

Rognon sauté Jean Sans Peur   11.50
(Sauteed veal kidneys in mustard and cream sauce, with mushrooms)

Gigot rôti aux flageolets   11.50
(Roast leg of lamb with flageolets beans)

Cassoulet Toulousain   13.50
(Goose, lamb, pork and white beans baked in casserole)

Entrecôte Sauté sauce poivrade   12.50
(Sirloin Steak with pepper sauce)

La Douzaine d'Escargots Bourguignonne   10.50
(One dozen of Snails baked in shells with garlic butter)

+ ___Our Daily Specials___

123

Palatine
LE TITI DE PARIS
French

$$$

French food, while often expensive, need not be served in an atmosphere of stuffiness (translate snobbishness) to be successful. A case in point is Le Titi de Paris. The name of the restaurant—loosely translated, "Parisian rascal"—perfectly captures the pixie-like quality of owner and maître d' Christian, and his personality is stamped on the restaurant; the ambience is pleasant and friendly if not intimate. The cuisine is the finest, and the main course selections are a gourmet's delight. Ris de veau Normande combines calvados with sweetbreads and mushrooms in a fine preparation. Lamb chops are delicately herbed so as not to mask the unmistakable character of the meat itself. Roast duckling comes with a crackling crisp skin in a peach sauce that offers a refreshing change from the bigarade or Montmorency so commonly found elsewhere. Seafood selections are also prepared with a connoisseur's touch. Soups, the true test of a restaurant kitchen, are often in a class by themselves. Daily specials not shown on the menu, but selected on the basis of availability of ingredients, round out the splendid offerings. A luncheon menu offers many of the dinner items at substantially lower cost.

LE TITI DE PARIS, 2275 Rand Road, Palatine. Telephone: 359-4434. Lunch: 11:30 am-2:30 pm, Tuesday-Friday. Dinner: 5:30 pm-10:30 pm, Tuesday-Friday; 5 pm-midnight, Saturday; 3 pm-11 pm, Sunday. Closed Monday. Cards: BA, MC. Reservations required. Parking in adjacent lot. Full bar. service; excellent wine list.

Our Specialties

Tarte Niçoise

Bisque de Homard

Filet of Dover Sole d'Antin

Canard Rôti aux Pêches

Poitrine de Volaille Nantaise

Gâteau Maison

Entrеés et Grillades

Entrecôte Marchand de vin 9 25

N.Y. sirloin steak broiled, served with a light red wine sauce and diced shallots.

Côtes D'agneau aux herbes de Provence 9 50

Double lamb chops broiled with herbs of southern France.

Filet les Trois Dauphins 9 25

Tenderloin filet broiled, served with a light sauce bearnaise, diced tomatoes and herbs.

Steak au Poivre 10 50

N.Y. sirloin steak saute with fresh ground pepper, flambe with cognac in a reduction of veal stock and herbs.

Poitrine de volaille Nantaise 7 75

Boneless breast of chicken saute served with rice, fresh seafood sauce, cheese au gratin.

Médaillon de veau Valleé d'Auge 9 25

Thin scalopini of veal saute served with fresh apple slices, calvados.

Canard Rôti aux Pêches 8 75

Roast duckling with peach sauce and herbs.

Ris de veau Normande 9 50

Sweetbread saute served with a light white wine sauce, calvados, and sliced fresh mushrooms.

Rognons de veau Bercy 7 25

Veal kidney saute and flambe with cognac, served with a light white wine sauce and diced shallots.

Calf's liver Lyonnaise 7 75

Calf's liver saute with butter and onions.

LES OEUFS
Omelettes

$

Just a few steps off the magnificent mile, tucked next to the lobby in the Playboy Towers, is one of the more intriguing restaurants in Chicago. Les Oeufs specializes in omelettes and other egg entrées. Humpty Dumpty never had it so good, whether your taste is for a fairly simple omelette Florentine or for the "customer's choice" omelette, where you decide what goes into the works. The omelette veronique is one of my favorites. Large bits of chicken and sautéed fresh mushroom slices are complemented by white seedless grapes in a wine sauce. The ratatouille omelette gives a new twist to the classic French vegetable preparation. Most selections include soup or salad from the salad bar. A limited choice of wines and a full range of cocktails are offered. The surroundings leave nothing to be desired, with lots of open space, comfortable seating and Mexican tile accents. Service is generally good.

LES OEUFS, 163 East Walton (in the Playboy Towers), Chicago. Telephone: 751-8100. Hours: 11 am-11 pm, Tuesday-Friday; 10 am-midnight, Saturday and Sunday; closed Monday. Cards: AE, BA, CB, DC, MC. No reservations. Valet parking. Full bar service.

Chicago and Suburbs
THE MAGIC PAN
Crêpes $

Imported from San Francisco, The Magic Pan Crêperies have become real Chicago favorites. The specialties are crêpes and their Hungarian cousins, palacsintas. Chicago's first Magic Pan at 60 East Walton set the style for the others which have sprung up in local shopping centers. That style is in the fashion of a French country house with use of wood, bare brick, greenery and open spaces. The Magic Pan, by the way, pioneered crêpe making on the outside bottom of the pan; it is part of the experience to go up to the open-sided preparation area and see their patented method. But the real story, of course, is the food. The crêpes are uniformly rich and filling. All stuffings except for the spinach soufflé (which comes from Stouffer's) are prepared from scratch. Seafood crêpes are especially luscious. Desserts satisfy the most demanding sweet tooth.

THE MAGIC PAN CRÊPERIE, 60 East Walton, Chicago. Telephone: 943-2456. Hours: 11 am-midnight, Monday-Thursday; until 1 am Friday and Saturday; until 9 pm Sunday. Suburban locations: Hawthorn Center, Vernon Hills; Woodfield Center, Schaumbert; Old Orchard Center, Skokie; Oak Brook Center, Oak Brook; and Orland Square, Orland Park. All suburban locations open 11 am-10 pm, Monday-Thursday; until midnight Friday and Saturday; until 9 pm Sunday. Cards: AE, BA, DC, MC. No reservations. Free parking for suburban locations. Full bar service; house wine by glass or carafe.

Chicago
MATEGRANO'S
Italian

$$

A few blocks' stretch along West Taylor Street on the Near
Southwest Side is a remnant of a once much larger Italian
neighborhood which existed before heavy construction
took its toll. Small markets, Italian ice stands and a sprin-
kling of Italian restaurants still contribute a special char-
acter. One of those restaurants is Mategrano's. The style is
Neapolitan with emphasis on seafood specialties such as
baccala (codfish, not always available), calamari and octo-
pus. Pastas are homemade in the family-related bakery
down the street. Three sisters and their brother, who tends
the bar, cater to regulars and newcomers alike with a warm
welcome. Mategrano's is famous for its special Thursday
and Saturday night buffets, real dining adventures for $3.95
per person. This all-you-care-to-eat experience is a great
opportunity to sample a wide array of Italian foods—far
beyond spaghetti and meatballs.

MATEGRANO'S, 1321 West Taylor Street, Chicago. Tele-
phone: 243-8441. Hours: 11 am-9:30 pm, Tuesday-Friday;
4 pm-10 pm, Saturday and Sunday; closed Monday. Cards:
AE, BA. Reservations suggested. Free parking in adjacent
lot. Full bar service.

Italian Dishes

SPAGHETTI OR MOSTACCIOLI	3.00
SPAGHETTI OR MOSTACCIOLI WITH MEAT BALL OR SAUSAGE	3.60
BAKED LASAGNA WITH MEAT BALL OR SAUSAGE	4.75
FETTUCCINE, Red Gravy	3.50
FETTUCCINE WITH MEAT BALL OR SAUSAGE	4.00
FETTUCCINE AL ALFREDO (Cheese and Butter)	3.75
HOME-MADE CHEESE RAVIOLI	3.25
HOME-MADE CHEESE RAVIOLI WITH MEAT BALL OR SAUSAGE	4.50
HOME-MADE MEAT RAVIOLI	3.75
HOME-MADE MEAT RAVIOLI WITH MEAT BALL OR SAUSAGE	4.50
HOME-MADE CAVATELLI	3.25
HOME-MADE CAVATELLI WITH MEAT BALL OR SAUSAGE	4.75
LINGUINI OR SPAGHETTI AL AGLIO OLIO (Oil and Garlic Sauce)	3.25
LINGUINI OR SPAGHETTI WITH CLAM SAUCE (Red or White)	4.25
HOME-MADE MANICOTTI	3.75
HOME-MADE MANICOTTI WITH MEAT BALL OR SAUSAGE	4.50
SPAGHETTI WITH MUSHROOM SAUCE	3.75
SPAGHETTI WITH ANCHOVIES	4.25

Above Orders Include: Salad, Bread and Butter

Specialties of the House

FRETTA: Combination of a Green Vegetable and Egg Pan Fried, with Meat Balls or Sausage	2.95
PASTA FAGIOLI	2.25
ESCAROLE AND BEANS	2.25
TRIPPA (Tripe with Tomato Sauce)	2.75
CALAMARA with Spaghetti (Squid)	3.25
POLPI with Spaghetti (Octopus)	3.25
BRACIOLE BREGILIANO, Mostaccioli and Salad (Flank Steak Rolled)	5.50
EGG PLANT PARMIGIANA AND MOSTACCIOLI (Egg Plant with Moscella Cheese), Salad	4.75

Steaks and Chops

NEW YORK STRIP STEAK with Onions	5.50
BROILED LAMB LOIN with Vegetable	5.50

Above Orders Include: Salad and Mostaccioli or Spaghetti

Veal Dishes

VEAL AL LEMONE	5.75
VEAL PARMIGIANA	5.75
VEAL SCALLOPINI	5.75
BREADED VEAL CUTLET	5.75

Above Orders Include: Mostaccioli and Salad

BROILED CHOPPED SIRLOIN with Onions, Salad and Mostaccioli	3.00
LASAGNA DINNER WITH MEAT BALL OR SAUSAGE and Salad	4.75

129

Waukegan
MATHON'S
Seafood

$$

About 45 miles north of Chicago, Mathon's reputation for good fresh lake fish is widely known around the area. The restaurant was opened years ago by the late Mathon Kyritsis and is still run by his family. Mathon achieved coast-to-coast fame by his weather predictions: If the perch are fat and swim deep in Lake Michigan, expect a cold winter. Perch is a house specialty, fresh from the Lake, sweet and succulent in a golden brown deep-fried batter crust. Smelt is an equally popular specialty, but apart from

---

• *Fresh Fish from the Great Lakes*

LAKE SMELT (Deep Fried)............................ 4.25
Locally caught

FILLET OF LAKE PERCH (Deep Fried) 5.25

TENDERLOIN OF TROUT (Tartar Sauce) 5.35
Cut in strips and deep fried

LAKE TROUT (Broiled or Pan Fried) 5.65

WHITEFISH (Broiled or Pan Fried) 5.65
Shipped direct to us from Lake Superior

PLANKED TROUT 6.25
Broiled on oak plank and garnished with mashed potatoes

PLANKED WHITEFISH 6.25
Broiled on oak plank and garnished with mashed potatoes

RAINBOW TROUT (Pan Fried) 5.55
From Silver Springs Trout Farm

• *Sea Food from the Coast*

WHOLE, MAINE LOBSTER – 2¼ Lbs. .... P.O.R.
Broiled — Steamed only when requested

SHRIMPS, FRENCH FRIED, A LA MATHON'S 6.45
A very unusual delicacy ... Try it!

Great Lakes fish, I also recommend scallops, Dover sole almondine or fried oysters. Featured for dessert is home-made graham cracker cream pie; other dessert choices are untypically ordinary.

MATHON'S, 6 Clayton, Waukegan. Telephone: 662-3610. Hours: 11 am-9:30 pm, Tuesday-Thursday; until 10:30 Friday and Saturday; noon-8:30 pm, Sunday; closed Monday. Cards: AE, BA, CB, DC, MC. Reservations accepted. Free parking in adjacent lot. Full bar service.

KING CRAB LEGS 8.50
Alaska's Finest

COMBINATION SEA FOOD PLATTER (Deep Fried) 6.15
Shrimps, Scallops, Oysters, Fillet of Sole, Tenderloin of Trout, and Smelt

BROILED AFRICAN LOBSTER TAIL (Drawn Butter) 11.95
A most popular American dish

LOBSTER THERMIDOR 9.95
Served in a very delightful manner

SCALLOPS, GENUINE (Deep Fried) (Tartar Sauce).... 6.25

WHOLE DOVER SOLE (Sauteed in Butter) (Almondine)... 7.85
Something new — highly recommended

OUR HALF AND HALF SPECIAL 6.45
Scallops and French Fried Shrimp

FRIED OYSTERS (Tartar Sauce) 5.75
Served in season from September to April

FILLET OF SOLE (Tartar Sauce) 4.65
Boneless, recommended for children

SOFT SHELL CRABS (Tartar Sauce) 6.65
A Chesapeake Bay delicacy

LOUISIANA FROG LEGS (Tartar Sauce) 6.65

SHAD ROE (Sautéed in Butter) 8.25
Highly recommended

HALIBUT STEAK (Fried) 4.75
Boneless, recommended for children
ALMONDINE WITH ABOVE ORDERS 50¢ EXTRA

Chicago
MATSUYA
Japanese

$

This is one of the dozens of little finds that dot Clark Street. There is nothing on Matsuya's menu I have not found at other Japanese restaurants, but everything I have tasted is exceptional. You can order à la carte or from special combinations. Either way, it is difficult to spend more than $5 to $6 per person. From the appetizer selection, choose spinach in a soy-based sesame sauce for $1. The spinach is cold, the sauce delicately sweet and salty. Matsuya does a fine job with fish, charcoal broiled with crisp skin. Fish varies depending on what is fresh; pike and mackerel are common selections. Broiled eel is for adventurous diners; sashimi, the popular dish of raw tuna, is another tempting offering. Combination dinners offer a taste of this and that, including delicately batter-coated tempura shrimp and vegetables, beef teriyaki and sashimi for $5.45. All dinners include a small cabbage salad, excellent clear hot broth, rice, light green tea with a delicate wood-like fragrance, and dessert.

MATSUYA, 3469 North Clark Street, Chicago. Telephone: 248-2677. Hours: 5 pm-10 pm, Monday-Friday; noon-10 pm, Saturday and Sunday. No cards. Reservations accepted. Street parking. Small choice of wines and saki only.

SASHIMI (filet of fresh tuna, sea
    bass or yellow tail on a bed of
    shredded raw cabbage with
    wasabi—Japanese horseradish)   4.25

TEMPURA (deep fried crispy butter-
    fly fresh shrimp and assorted
    vegetables)   3.50

TERIYAKI-FISH (charcoal broiled
    fresh mackerel, salmon, spanish
    mackerel, butterfish, sanma,
    etc. with marinated sauce)   3.25

SHOI-YAKI (charcoal broiled
    above fresh fish)   3.25

NIZAKANA (the above fresh fish
    cooked in special sauce)   3.50

UNAGI-KABAYAKI (charcoal
    broiled eel)   5.75

CHIRI-NABE (casserole dish with
    white chipped fish and assorted
    vegetables in broth, served with
    special dipping sauce)   2.95

YOSE-NABE (casserole dish with
    chipped white fish, fish cake
    and assorted vegetables and
    noodles in broth   3.25

TUNA-TEMPURA (deep fried
    chipped tuna and assorted
    vegetables)   3.50

OROSHI-AE (chipped filet of
    fresh tuna with Japanese
    grated radish and marinated
    horseradish sauce)   3.95

Chicago
MAXIM'S DE PARIS
French

$$$

Time races on elsewhere, but at Maxim's the fin de siècle atmosphere remains. Although a Chicago establishment only since 1964, its mirrors and dark woods have a patina of aged grandeur. Diners are served by tuxedoed waiters and serenaded by a string ensemble. Maxim's recommends its own house specialties; I will not presume to know better than they, except to recommend the fine turbot, delicate veal kidneys and lovely veal Orloff. The à la carte menu is extensive and expensive. The excellent wine list meets the demands of the fine food. Maxim's de Paris in Chicago serves the best of traditional French haute cuisine.

MAXIM'S DE PARIS, 1300 North Astor, Chicago. Telephone: 943-1136. Lunch: noon-3 pm, Monday-Saturday. Dinner: 6 pm-1 am, Monday-Sunday. Cards: AE, BA, CB, DC, MC. Reservations required. Parking in adjacent garage. Full bar service.

SPECIALITES DE MAXIM'S

Pate de Grives au Myrte 8.00
Pate of Thrush

Pate de Merles au Cognac 8.00
Pate of Blackbird

Billi Bi (chaud ou froid)   2.95
Cream of Mussels Soup (hot or cold)

Truite au Bleu, Sauce Hollandaise 8.75
Fresh Mountain Trout, poached, with Hollandaise sauce

Coquilles St. Jacques aux Petits Legumes 8.75

Homard a la Nage 14.75
Whole poached Maine Lobster served in its own broth

Escalope Saumon a l' Oseille 9.75
Salmon with Sorrel Sauce

Escalopines de Veau au Vermouth 9.50
Slices of Veal, in a sauce of Vermouth,
tomatoes and mushrooms

Poulet saute au Xeres 7.75
Chicken saute in Sherry Wine

Chicago
MILLER'S PUB
American

$$

Here is the kind of place that can draw an after-theater crowd, the cop on the beat, or anyone who is just plain hungry at almost any hour of the day or night. Miller's late-night (or early-morning, if you prefer) hours make it a natural magnet for diners or snackers in the Loop. There's lots of imitation stained glass, vinyl seating and heavy use of wood, creating a congenial rather than elegant atmosphere. Miller's Pub is noted for its baby back ribs and its steaks. I particularly like the 12-ounce sirloin butt which satisfies a hearty appetite for dinner or a late-night snack. There is a sprinkling of Greek dishes and some Italian fare on the menu. Miller's Pub may be trying to be all things to all people; it fairly well succeeds.

MILLER'S PUB, 23 East Adams, Chicago. Telephone: 922-7446. Hours: 7 am-4 am, daily. Cards: AE, BA, CB, DC, MC. No reservations. Parking at Adams-State Garage (at discount for dinner). Full bar service.

BROILED CHICKEN
ATHENIAN STYLE
Greek Salad
Potato or Pilaf
4.95

PASTICHIO
Baked Macaroni
Meat Pie
The House Specialty
Served with Greek
Salad Bowl
4.50

GREEK STYLE
LAMB CHOPS
Choice of
Potato or Pilaf
Greek Salad
8.75

From Our Blazing Broiler

BAR-B-Q CANADIAN BABY BACK RIBS,
Salad Bowl or Creamy Cole Slaw,
Choice of Potato **6.95**

PRIME NEW YORK CUT STEAK, 16 Oz., Onion Rings 8.95
FILET MIGNON, Mushroom Caps 12 oz. 8.95
LADIES FILET MIGNON, Mushroom Caps 8 oz. 6.95
"MILLER'S" PRIME SIRLOIN BUTT STEAK, Onion Rings 12 oz. 7.50
JUNIOR "MILLER'S" PRIME BUTT STEAK 8 oz. 5.95
TWO CENTER CUT PORK CHOPS..................... 5.95
3 DOUBLE THICK LAMB CHOPS 7.95
HALF BROILED CHICKEN 4.25
CHOPPED SIRLOIN STEAK, Mushroom Sauce 4.25

The Above Orders Include Salad Bowl and Choice of Potatoes
Small Athenian Salad .75 extra — Roquefort Dressing .50 extra

THE KING AND
THE LADY
8 oz. Filet Mignon
Plus
7 oz. Baby Lobster Tail
Choice of Potato
Salad Bowl
11.50

ROAST PRIME RIBS
OF BEEF, Au Jus
Choice of Potato
Veg. - Salad Bowl
Diamond Jim Brady Cut
7.95
(Lillian Russell Cut)
6.95

PEPPER STEAK
Spicy Beef Tenderloin
Sauté en Casserole
Salad Bowl
Potato or Pilaf
7.50

PRIME BEEF TIPS
EN BROCHETTE
Potato or Pilaf
Salad Bowl
6.25

SOUTHERN FRIED
CHICKEN
Choice of Potato
Salad Bowl
4.25

CHICKEN "KIEV"
Chicken Gravy
Potato or Pilaf
Salad Bowl
5.25

137

MILL RACE INN
American $$

The Fox River flows quietly by. When the wind blows, tree limbs brush against the window panes. Outside, you can feed the ducks with chunks of homemade bread. This is the Mill Race Inn. The Inn was not always so. Nearly 125 years ago there was a blacksmith's shop on the site where the restaurant now stands. In fact, one of the old limestone walls of the smithy's shack is incorporated into the restaurant's design. Today, the Inn occupies five dining rooms seating about 170 people. The food is basic American and although the menu changes daily, there are some regulars. You'll always find prime rib of beef, the kind of fare which, in the words of Thomas Wolfe, you can "pillory a tooth on." Braised lamb shank and oven-baked chicken are other house specialties. You won't find any steaks or deep-fried foods, but you can occasionally find turkey Parmesan with broccoli, sautéed filet of sole, and braised short ribs of beef. À la carte desserts, all homemade, include deep-dish apple pie with cinnamon ice cream, figs and wine in frozen cream, strawberry rhubarb crême and tapioca pudding. Complete dinner prices range from $5.45 to $7.95. Luncheon offerings run from about $2.75 to $5.25 and, like the dinners, change daily. A new addition to the Inn is a screened gazebo; in fair weather you can sit outside and watch the river and its ducks flow past. Incidentally, the Mill Race Inn does have a dress code which requires gentlemen to wear jackets at dinner.

MILL RACE INN, 4 East State Street, Geneva. Telephone: 232-2030. Hours: 11:45 am-3 pm, Tuesday-Saturday; 5:30 pm-8:30 pm, Tuesday-Thursday; 5:30 pm-9 pm, Friday and Saturday; 11:30 am-8:30 pm, Sunday; closed Mondays, most major holidays and the entire month of February. Cards: AE, BA, MC. Reservations suggested. Free parking in adjacent lots. Full bar service. Jackets required at dinner.

Chicago
MIOMIR'S
Serbian

$$

Food, Balkan wines and an ethnic floor show all add up to a sparkling evening of fun. Miomir, the smiling Serb in a dark, double-breasted suit, graciously greets his patrons and sees to their comforts. This is more than a restaurant; it is an event, a happening, a wedding feast. There is so much joy and good fun here that the walls practically burst. Family-style dinners at $9.75 include a sampling of probably everything in the kitchen. Be sure to have the house appetizers, kajmak (a goat's milk cheese spread) and ajvar (eggplant, mild green peppers and seasonings in an olive oil base). The house soup, a vegetable broth with veal, is topnotch. If you like shish kebab, try the Serbian kind, made with pork tenderloin. Other grilled specialties include ground veal and beef shaped into sausage-like links called cevapcici. Pleskavica is a ground steak of veal, beef and a bit of lamb sautéed in olive oil with red peppers and onions. Muckalica is similar but more highly seasoned. The food is only part of the story at Miomir's, where a six-piece band sings in 16 languages. As moderate as are the prices, dinners are 15 percent less on Wednesday and Thursday and that includes the entertainment.

MIOMIR'S SERBIAN CLUB, 2255 West Lawrence, Chicago. Telephone: 784-2111. Hours: 5 pm-2 am, Sunday and Wednesday-Friday; until 3 am Saturday; closed Monday and Tuesday. Cards: BA, MC. Reservations suggested, especially weekends. Street parking; nearby lot. Full bar service.

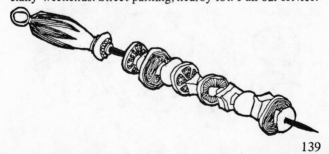

Chicago
NANTUCKET COVE
Seafood

$$

You often hear people say that Chicago is a great steak town. While that certainly is true, it is also true that we don't do so badly where seafood is concerned. Among the city's more prominent seafood specialty houses is Nantucket Cove. This restaurant has a truly distinctive atmosphere so salty that you might think you should wear a sou'wester to keep high and dry. It's the kind of place where Billy Bigelow might go for a drink and a bucket of steamers after a hard night's work on the carousel. The restaurant, which seats 210 diners, is loaded with period pieces evoking the last century's great days of whaling. If our waiter had introduced himself by saying, "Call me Ishmael," I wouldn't have been too shocked. Among the excellent selections is flounder stuffed with crab meat. The fish is rich and clean tasting; the crab meat stuffing is accented with wine sauce. The fritter-fried shrimp dinner yields a half dozen of the little fellows. From time to time, Nantucket Cove has a special lobster dinner which came in for about $6.50 at this writing; but you'd better check on the price when you visit.

NANTUCKET COVE, 1000 North Lake Shore Drive, Chicago. Telephone: 943-1600. Hours: 5 pm-1 am, daily. Cards: BA, MC. Reservations suggested. Parking available at discount. Full bar service.

Appetizers

OYSTERS ON THE HALF SHELL (6) . . 2.25
CHERRYSTONE CLAMS (6) 2.25
STEAMED CLAMS (12) 2.25
CRABMEAT COCKTAIL 2.50
NANTUCKET TURTLE SOUP with Sherry . .95
CREAMY CLAM CHOWDER 95
ONION SOUP au Gratin 95
OYSTERS ROCKEFELLER (4) 2.25

Dinner

TINY BAY SCALLOPS SAUTE 5.95
FLOUNDER STUFFED WITH CRABMEAT . . . 6.75
FILET OF SALMON, HOLLANDAISE 7.95
POMPANO STUFFED WITH
      CRABMEAT HOLLANDAISE 8.25
SHRIMP: FRITTER-FRIED, Sauce Tartare 5.95
      NEWBURG 6.25
STUFFED DEVILED CRAB 6.75
DOVER SOLE 8.95
ALASKAN KING CRAB LEGS 7.95

Lobsters

Ours are not simply alive, but are handled in such a manner that they are their natural ferocious selves.
Pick one from the pond (or watch the waiters do it) and you'll see the difference. We can't divulge our
secret, but it makes such a difference in taste and texture that we serve more than a ton of them a week.
All are steamed unless you tell us otherwise.

ONE CHICKEN LOBSTER: For the Petite Appetite 8.95
MEDIUM SIZE WHOLE LOBSTER 13.95
TWO ONE POUND LOBSTERS: For the Hearty Appetite 15.95
BAKED STUFFED LOBSTER SAVANNAH 8.95
NANTUCKET PLATTER: One-Pound Lobster, Fried Shrimp and Clams . 9.95
NEW ENGLAND BEACH PARTY CLAMBAKE (FOR TWO):
Two One-Pound Lobsters, Steamed Clams, Shrimp in Shell, Yams, and Corn on the
Cob, Covered in Seaweed and Baked in Earthern Casserole 19.50

LARGE SHRIMP, Chilled Cocktail or Steamed in Beer 2.25
CEVICHE NANTUCKET: A Spicy Variety of Marinated Fish 1.15

Trout

CHARCOAL BROILED 6.25
SAUTE AMANDINE 6.50
STUFFED WITH CRABMEAT AND WRAPPED IN VINE LEAVES 7.75

From The Charcoal Broiler

LAND AND SEAS – Sirloin Steak & Lobster Tail 11.95

FILET OF RED SNAPPER . . . . 7.50   CAPTAIN'S SIRLOIN STEAK 8.95
POMPANO . . . . 7.75   MATE'S SIRLOIN STEAK 7.95
WHITE FISH . . . . 7.25   FILET MIGNON 8.75
LOBSTER TAIL . . . . 8.50   CHOPPED BEEF STEAK 5.50

ALA CARTE – GREEN BEANS, CAULIFLOWER, JUNE PEAS OR CORN ON COB . . .95

All Entrees are served with Baked Potato and Tossed Green Salad. Choice of our Original Nantucket
Creamy or Italian Dressings. "Our own Pilgrim Cornsticks" are freshly baked.

Children Served One Half Order of Shrimp; Chopped Beef, Potato & Salad 3.25

Chicago
THE NINETY-FIFTH
French $$$

Although The Ninety-Fifth is a luxury restaurant which takes up the entire ninety-fifth floor of the John Hancock Center (plus the ninety-sixth if you include the Sybaris Lounge), it has had its ups and downs since it opened a few years ago. The Ninety-Fifth is huge, seating 225 or more people. Its size is its worst enemy; the problems created by preparing and serving à la carte French dinners to that many people are enormous. Yet, when it is good, The Ninety-Fifth is very, very good. And more often than not it is very good; not great perhaps, but very good. A fairly new menu displays ambitious goals. Frogs legs sautéed in butter sauce, sweetbreads braised in Madeira, poached salmon with champagne and sorrel sauces would test the excellence of any French kitchen. Soups, such as the consommé, show real traces of the chef's art, especially where elegant simplicity is appreciated. The sauces are delicate, portions are large, and the three courses (appetizer or soup, entrée accompanied by vegetables, and dessert) will bountifully satisfy. The wine list is long and handsomely presented in a leather-bound volume. Some rare selections from the Dr. Barolet Collection are included. The view from The Ninety-Fifth is the most glorious in Chicago. It *is* Chicago, the suburbs and the Lake stretching off to the horizons. Try to arrive for cocktails at sunset and ask for a table with the western view for a spectacular and awe-inspiring display. Check your almanac for show times.

THE NINETY-FIFTH, 875 North Michigan Avenue (in the John Hancock Center, Chestnut Street entrance), Chicago. Telephone: 787-9596. Lunch: noon-3 pm, Monday-Saturday. Dinner: 6 pm-midnight, Monday-Saturday; 6 pm-10 pm Sunday. Sunday brunch: 11:30 am-3 pm. Cards: AE, BA, CB, DC, MC. Reservations required. Parking in building garage. Full bar service.

the ninety-fifth

 LES POISSONS ET CRUSTACES

HOMARD THERMIDOR 14.75
Lobster Cooked in White Wine with Aromatic Herbs

SAUMON POCHE A L'OSEILLE 9.00
Poached Salmon with a Champagne Sauce and Sorrel

FILET DE TURBOTIN FLORENTINE 10.00
Poached Fillet of Turbot on Leaf Spinach with Mushrooms

SOLE DE DOUVRES MEUNIERE 10.25
Imported Dover Sole Sauteed in Butter and Lemon

TRUITE GRENOBLOISE 8.50
Mountain Trout sauteed with Butter, Lemon and Capers

POISSON FRAIS DU MARCHE 7.75
Fresh Fish from the Market

 LES VIANDES

LE COQ CHARLEMAGNE 8.50
Chicken in Red Burgundy Wine, Pearl Onions,
Bacon, Mushrooms and Croutons

CAILLES A LA VIGNERONNE 8.25
Quail in Champagne Sauce with
peeled White Grapes

RIS DE VEAU FINANCIERE 9.25
Sweetbreads braised in Madeira with
Truffles, Mushrooms and Olives

STEAK DIANE 11.75
Mignonettes of Beef
prepared at Your Table

CANETON ROTI AU POIVRE DES ISLES 10.00
Roast Duckling with Imported Green Peppercorns

NOISETTE DE VEAU AUX MORILLES 12.25
Milk-Fed Veal sauteed with Imported Wild Mushrooms

TOURNEDOS BEAUGENCY 12.50
Beef Tenderloin Served with
Beef Marrow and Artichoke Bottoms

ENTRECOTE AUX CEPES 12.00
Sirloin Steak served with
Imported Wild Mushrooms

CARRE D'AGNEAU PERSILLE (For Two) 25.00
Roast Rack of Lamb with an Array of Fresh Vegetables

 LA VOITURE

LE FILET DE BOEUF WELLINGTON 12.25
Served with Fresh Whole String Beans, Potatoes and Sauce Perigourdine

 LES GRILLADES

FILET MIGNON GRILLE BEARNAISE 11.75
Center Cut of Tenderloin, Bearnaise Sauce

COTES D'AGNEAU VERT PRE 12.00
Grilled Lamb Chops with Maitre d' Butter

ENTRECOTE AUX SENTEURS DE PROVENCE 11.50
Broiled Strip Sirloin with Herb Flavored Butter

CHATEAUBRIAND BOUQUETIERE (For Two) 25.00
Broiled Double Tenderloin with Bearnaise Sauce and an Array of Fresh Vegetables

DOUBLE ENTRECOTE GRILLEE CECILIA (For Two) 24.50
Broiled Double Sirloin with Bearnaise Sauce and an Array of Fresh Vegetables

Chicago
NORTHERN CHINA
Chinese (Mandarin) $$

There has been an explosion of Mandarin-style restaurants in the city and suburbs in recent years. Most of the fallout has been good. One of the newest and best is Northern China. You wouldn't think this was anything special to drive by and look at the exterior. In fact the dining room itself is not particularly lavish, but since you don't eat the wallpaper, it is not all that critical. The Mandarin food prepared here seems to have a character all its own, compared to other such restaurants that I know. For one thing, seasonings are more pronounced. For instance, sizzling rice soup is noticeably peppered. Among appetizers, the steamed pot stickers, which have a delicate flavor, are best eaten in a soy-based sauce which works beautifully by supplementing its own complex flavorings with the dumplings and their meat fillings. Among main course selections, I like the snow peas and black mushrooms. The peas retain a delicate crispness which contrasts nicely with the silky sensuality of the mushrooms. Both are nicely worked in a lightly salted sauce. If you don't have the opportunity to phone a day in advance for Peking duck, try the diced chicken in plum sauce. At the least, you'll get the tart pleasure of hoisin sauce combined with flavorful chunks of chicken meat. Seafood dishes retain proper textures which can be lost from too much stir-frying in less sensitive hands. Among desserts, the glazed fruits are scrumptious, especially the pepa, which are similar to apricots or peaches.

NORTHERN CHINA, 5601 North Clark Street, Chicago. Telephone: 334-8194. Hours: 11:30 am-10 pm, Monday-Thursday; until 11 pm Friday and Saturday; noon-9 pm, Sunday. Cards: AE, BA, DC, MC. Reservations accepted. Street parking. No alcoholic beverages; you may bring your own.

SEA FOOD

THREE INGREDIENTS 4.95
Seasonal choice of abalone, shrimps, sea cucumbers or sea scallops, delicately blended and sauted.

SAUTEED "HAPPY FAMILY" 4.95
Assorted sea food with vegetables, also called "The Eight Delicacies"

FRIED SHRIMP 4.00

SWEET AND SOUR SHRIMP 4.25

SHRIMP WITH GREEN PEAS 4.25

CURRY SHRIMP 4.25

OYSTER SAUCE ABALONE 4.95

SIZZLING RICE SHRIMP 4.25
Sauteed shrimp in sweet and sour sauce of tomatoes with sizzling golden rice crust

PRINCESS PRAWNS 4.50
Deep fried large prawns blended with our special hot sauce

BRAISED SEA CUCUMBERS . . . . (Seasonal)
Choice imported sea cucumbers braised with green onions

SHRIMP WITH EGGS 4.00

SNOW PEAS WITH SHRIMP 4.75

MUSHROOMS, BAMBOO SHOOTS WITH SHRIMP 4.75

HOT BRAISED FISH . . . . Seasonal
Whole, fresh Red Snapper (prepared) with finely chopped waterchestnuts, mushrooms, bamboo shoots, hot pepper and our special plum sauce. Seasonal.

SWEET AND SOUR FISH . . . . (Seasonal)

STEAMED FISH . . . . Seasonal
Whole, fresh fish garnished with a blend of mushrooms, sliced ham and seasoned with oriental condiments. Seasonal.

Chicago
NEW JAPAN
Japanese

$

Easy to miss if you don't look closely, New Japan is tucked into a small storefront around the corner from busy Rush Street, in the midst of a swinging singles bar area. A tasteful use of wood and glass creates the hint of Japanese atmosphere, just enough to offset the look of coffee shop basic. There are half a dozen or so tables plus a row of counter stools. But you don't come here for an authentic tea ceremony. You come for some excellent, although not unusual, Japanese food. Egg rolls are 39 cents each, ditto for fried chicken wings served so piping hot they practically sputter on your plate. Ramen, a typical noodle broth from Japanese kitchens, is nothing short of delicious. Large-portioned tempura includes three big batter-dipped shrimp plus vegetables. Beef teriyaki is fine, but the pan-fried buckwheat noodles (yakisoba) are merely ordinary. New Japan is a penny diner's haven.

NEW JAPAN ORIENTAL CAFE, 45 West Division Street, Chicago. Telephone: 787-4248. Lunch: 11:45 am-2:30 pm, Monday-Saturday. Dinner: 5 pm-10 pm, Monday-Thursday; until 11 pm Friday and Saturday. Closed Sunday. No cards. No reservations. Street parking. No alcoholic beverages.

THE ORIGINAL PANCAKE HOUSE
Pancakes

$

Actually, "the" Original Pancake House is in Portland. The idea quickly spread eastward so that now in the greater Chicago area there are eight locations, with several more in the planning stage. Forget everything you know about pancake restaurants because none of them can touch the Original Pancake House. The big specialty is a huge apple pancake that practically overflows the edges of its serving platter. The pancake is really an oven cake, baked up almost like a soufflé, embedded with slices of tangy apple and served steaming hot with a luscious cinnamon glaze topping the crust. Another favorite is the 49'er flapjacks. These are old-fashioned chuckwagon pancakes, thin and gooey. The other pancakes are equally fine. This is a great place to come with the kids or with another couple or two. At some locations, the long wait for a table can be an annoyance, as they do not accept reservations. If you can, avoid weekend morning rush hours.

THE ORIGINAL PANCAKE HOUSE, 2020 North Lincoln Park West, Chicago. Telephone: 953-8130. Other locations in Chicago at 22 East Bellevue Place, 1516 East Hyde Park Boulevard and 10437 South Western Avenue. Suburban branches in Oak Forest, Wilmette, Villa Park and Naperville. Open for breakfast, lunch and dinner daily. No cards. No reservations. Parking available at reduced rates or free. No alcoholic beverages.

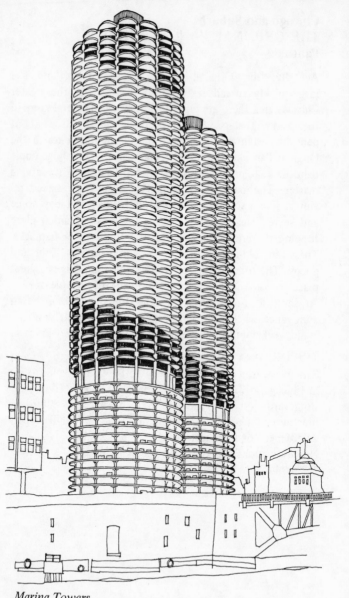

Marina Towers

Chicago
OSTIONERIA PLAYA AZUL
Mexican (Seafood)   **$**

The name roughly translated means Blue Point Oyster House, but oysters are only part of the menu. This is Mexican-style seafood, as different from the usual run of tacos and tortillas as black is from white. Located in the heart of the Pilsen community, Ostioneria Playa Azul is a neat storefront operation with furnishings out of Dinette City. The food is sensational. Several nautical salads, priced from $2.50 to $3.50, include oyster, shrimp, octopus, abalone and combinations. As delicious as these may be, don't miss ceviche for $3.75, a unique Mexican fish preparation. The fish is cut into chunks and marinated in lime juice for several hours; the citric acid in the juice literally cooks the fish. It is then mixed with avocado, tomatoes, onions and seasonings into a delicious cold salad. From the dinner section of the limited one-page menu you can order filet of white fish, red snapper, shrimp or lobster in any of several preparations. For instance, snapper Veracruzana for $5 comes with its crisp skin topped with bits of tomato, parsley, onion and avocado. It is snappy red snapper indeed. Almost everything else, except for the $9 grilled lobster, is in the $3.25 to $4 price range. Dinners include rice, a small salad and hot tortillas. By the way, the native tongue of the neighborhood is Spanish; if you have a hard time communicating what you want to your waitress, you can point to one of the several kinds of fish pictured on a decorative wall mural.

OSTIONERIA PLAYA AZUL, 1514 West 18th Street, Chicago. Telephone: 666-3033. Hours: 8 am-10 pm, Monday-Thursday; until 2 am, Friday and Saturday; until 11:30 pm Sunday. No cards. Reservations not necessary. Street parking. No alcoholic beverages; you may bring your own.

Chicago
THE PALLADION
Greek

$$

This is one of the Greek restaurants in Chicago which is patronized by Greeks. It is not uncommon to see whole families, from infants in arms to grandparents, gathered around a table until well past midnight. The attraction is not only the food, which is exceptional, but the lively Greek trio which helps transform the place into a night on the town in Athens. Ask for a selection of appetizers and enjoy mild Greek sausage, tender little meatballs sautéed in olive oil plus triangles of cheese and spinach in filo dough. As in other Greek restaurants, the combination plate offers the best bargain, but nothing is so expensive that you cannot choose what you want. Often served but not on the printed menu is lamb Exsohiko for $4.95. The chunks of lamb, artichokes, peas and kaseri cheese are baked in filo pastry and served steaming hot. Good wines are offered, but be like the regulars and order inexpensive Rodytis. Wine and other bar items cost more once the music gets under way.

THE PALLADION, 5035 North Lincoln Avenue, Chicago. Telephone: 271-4793. Hours: 11:30 am-4 am, Sunday-Friday; until 5 am Saturday. Cards: AE, BA, MC. Reservations suggested on weekends. Free parking lot. Full bar service.

GREEK SPECIALTIES

MOUSSAKA: Layers of eggplant, sautéed in butter, selected ground meat, potatoes, and topped with béchamel sauce $2.95

PASTITSIO: Mixed fresh spiced ground meat and macaroni, topped with creamy white sauce and parmesan cheese   2.95

DOLMADES AVGOLEMONO: Grape leaves stuffed with ground beef, lamb and rice, topped with egg lemon sauce   2.95

BRAISED LAMB, with rice and potatoes, or vegetable and potatoes   3.25

ROAST LEG OF LAMB: Sliced lamb with rice and potatoes, or vegetable and potatoes   3.45

ROAST BEEF: Sliced beef, with rice and potatoes, or vegetable and potatoes   3.45

ROAST CHICKEN, with rice and potatoes, or vegetable and potatoes   2.65

ROAST LOIN OF LAMB, with rice and potatoes, or vegetable and potatoes   2.45

SPECIALS OF THE HOUSE

PALLADION FAMILY PLATE FOR TWO OR MORE: Appetizer, saganaki, soup, salad, braised lamb, pastitsio, moussaka, dolmades, rice, potatoes, dessert and coffee PER PERSON   5.95

GIOUVETSI: Individual order of lamb cooked with rosa marina, spaghetti or noodles   3.25

PEPPER STEAK: Sliced beef tenderloin with pepper and mushrooms   5.95

COMBINATION PLATE: Braised lamb, pastitsio, dolmades, moussaka, rice and potatoes   3.75

FRIED GREEK SAUSAGE   2.65

FRIED LIVERS   2.65

FRIED GLYKADAKIA   4.75

Chicago
THE RITZ-CARLTON
Continental/French

$$$

The Ritz finally has shaken off its opening problems with service and is assuming the expected position of one of Chicago's finest restaurants. The formal à la carte French menu boasts some delicious and particularly unusual items such as saddle of antelope, quail stuffed with veal sweetbreads and truffled goose liver mousse, and roasted mallard with kiwi fruit. The dining room is elegant, although somewhat noisy; blame hardwood walls and poor acoustic planning. Service problems plagued The Ritz for several months after it first opened in early 1975. Now, fortunately, systems and procedures are working well. The dining room of the Ritz-Carlton is big-league entertaining.

THE RITZ-CARLTON DINING ROOM, 160 East Pearson Street (at Water Tower Place), Chicago. Telephone: 266-1000. Lunch: noon-2:30 pm, Monday-Saturday. Dinner: 6 pm-11:30 pm, daily. Cards: AE, BA, CB, DC, MC. Reservations required. Parking in hotel and building garages. Full bar service.

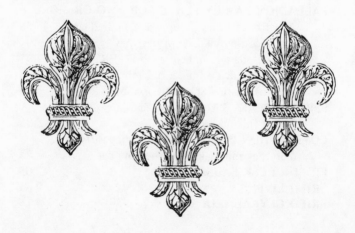

LES HORS D'OEUVRE FROIDS

Les Perles de Caviar Frais
Sur Glace, Blinis   14.50 (per ounce)
Beluga Caviar Presented on Ice Carving,
Served with Hot Blinis

Saumon Fumé Irlandais   6.00
Smoked Irish Salmon

Terrine de Ris de Veau aux Pistaches   3.75
Terrine of Veal Sweetbreads and Pistachio

Avocat Farci au Crabe et Caviar,
Sauce Moutarde   4.50
Stuffed Avocado with Crabmeat and Caviar,
Mustard Sauce

Huîtres Gratinées Bèarnaise,
Raymond Oliver   3.75
Fresh Oysters Glazed with Bèarnaise Sauce

Quenelles de Homard au Whiskey   4.50
Lobster Quenelles in Cream and Whiskey Sauce

Crêpe de Palourdes aux Épinards,
Hollandaise   3.25
Fresh Clams and Creamed Spinach Crêpe,
Flamed with Ricard, Glazed with Hollandaise

Pâté de Turbot aux Herbes de Provence,
Mousseline Nantua   3.75
Mousse of Turbot with Provences Herbs,
Light Lobster Sauce

Cocktail de Homard, Sauce Vincent   6.00
Half Lobster Cocktail Served in its Shell

Foie Gras Truffé   10.00
Truffled Foie Gras

Cornet de Saumon Fumé à la Gelée
d'Estragon   3.25
Mousse of Smoked Salmon with Tarragon Gelee

Terrine de Canard à l'Orange   3.25
Duckling Paté with Orange

Ragoût de Coquilles Saint-Jacques
aux Petits Légumes   3.75
Bay Scallops Simmered with Garden Vegetables

Petit Pâté Chaud de Gibier   4.50
Hot Venison Pâte in Crust (15 minutes)

Croustade d'Escargots aux Cêpes   5.50
Baked Snails Served in Pastry Croustade with
Cêpes Mushrooms, Garlic, Wine

LES POISSONS

Andouillette de Turbot Grillée,
Colman Sauce   9.50
Broiled Escalop of Turbot Stuffed with
Salmon Mousse, English Mustard Sauce

Suprêmes de Sole aux Bananes   9.50
Poached Filets of Dover Sole, with
Bananas and White Wine Sauce

Homard Grillé aux Deux Sauces   14.75
Broiled Lobster, Bearnaise and Nantua Sauces

Papillote de Saumon Frais,
Beurre Nantais   9.25
Suprême of Salmon with a fine Julienne of
Vegetable, Nantes Butter Sauce

Homard de nos Viviers, Sauté à la Corse   15.00
Fresh Lobster from our tanks,
Sauteed with Roe Sauce

Truite Farcie en Croûte, Sauce Amèricaine   9.50
Stuffed Trout in Crust, Lobster Sauce

LE GIBIER FRAIS

Noisettes de Chevreuil aux Baies
de Genièvre   13.75
Loin of Venison, Marinated in Wine, Sauteed and
Served with a Poivrade Sauce

Perdreau Rôti Sur Canapé   12.75
Roasted Young Partridge, Prepared Table Side

Selle d'Antilope Sautée, Grand Veneur   12.25
Boned Saddle of Antelope Sauteed,
with Grand Veneur Sauce

Canard Col-Vert aux Kiwis Frais
(For Two Only)   25.00
Roasted Mallard Duckling, with
Fresh Kiwis Fruits (25 minutes)

Albarine de Faisan Sauvage,
Grand Véfour   11.75
Crepinette of Wild Pheasant Filet with Foie Gras
and Truffle. Sauce Grand Véfour

LES ENTREES

Coeur de Filet au Poivre Vert, en Croûte   13.00
Center Cut of Tenderloin with
Green Peppercorn Sauce, in Crust

Caille en Caissette Ritz   14.50
Quail Stuffed with Veal Sweetbreads and
Truffled Goose Liver Mousse, Ivory Sauce

Pigeonneau Farci en Bécasse   12.50
Stuffed Baby Squab, Madeira Sauce

Civet de Canard à la Bourguignonne   10.50
Duckling Cooked in Red Wine with Tiny Onions,
Bacon, Mushrooms

Carré d'Agneau Poëllé, Bonne Femme
(For Two)   25.00
Roasted Rack of Lamb, Bonne Femme garniture
(20 minutes)

LES GRILLADES

Chateaubriand Bouquetière,
Sauce Bèarnaise (For Two)   26.00
Chateaubriand and its Bouquetière of Vegetables,
Bèarnaise Sauce (25 minutes)

Rouelle de Gigot d'Agneau Vert-Pré   9.75
Whole Slice of Leg of Lamb, Broiled and Served
with Bearnaise and Watercress

Côte de Veau aux Herbes de Provence   13.00
Veal Chop with Provence Herbs (20 minutes)

Brochette de Médaillons de Filet de Boeuf,
Sauce Madère   11.35
Medaillons of Beef Tenderloin in Brochette,
Madeira Sauce

Entrecôte Grillée Bordelaise Moutardée   12.50
Broiled Sirloin, Marrow and Mustard,
Bordelaise Sauce

T-Bone Steak Porterhouse (For Two)   27.00
Broiled T-Bone Steak (20 minutes)

Coeur de Filet Grillé, Sauce Foyot   12.50
Center Cut Tenderloin Steak, Foyot Sauce

Chicago
R.J. GRUNTS
American

$

This is the place that started the still continuing pattern of trendy, hip, Chicago restaurants. While not exactly an historical landmark yet, it is still a fun place to go. There are sandwiches, complete dinners, a salad bar, gooey desserts, wine and booze and good-looking waitresses. Expect good, solid fare, but nothing gourmet. Attack this place with gusto to experience anything but a conventional restaurant atmosphere.

R.J. GRUNTS, 2056 Lincoln Park West, Chicago. Telephone: 929-5363. Hours: 11:30 am-midnight, Monday-Thursday; until 1 am, Friday and Saturday; 2 pm-midnight, Sunday. Sunday brunch: 10 am-2 pm. No cards. No reservations. Parking in nearby garage (at discount). Full bar service.

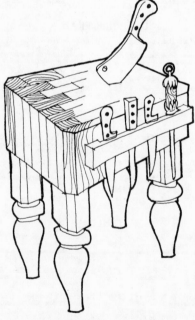

Chicago
SAUER'S
German/American $

Sauer's claims to be the only true brauhouse, or German "public house," in Chicago. I know of nothing else quite like it. In a huge building which has served duty as a school of the dance and as a warehouse, the restaurant has preserved the architectural integrity of the building. There are bare brick walls, a high, arched wood-beamed ceiling with skylights, and a pebble-aggregate concrete floor. At one end of the hall, which is almost half as long as a football field, is a raised stage on which live entertainment is presented on weekends. You can wet your whistle with mixed drinks, soft drinks or draft beer, light or dark. For food you can choose from one of six regular dinners or a fifth specialty of the day. The most expensive selection is a sirloin steak ($6.25) which weighs in at about six to eight ounces. Sauer's is primarily a beer and sandwiches place, although the daily specials are not to be dismissed too readily. I don't suggest that Sauer's has the best hamburger or corned beef and cabbage in town. But when you need someplace inexpensive on the Near South Side that can accommodate a large crowd or a small table of friends, it's a good place to do your eating and drinking. It's not a neighborhood tavern; it's a brauhouse.

SAUER'S, 311 East 23rd Street, Chicago. Telephone: 225-6171. Hours: 11 am-8 pm, Monday-Saturday; closed Sunday. No cards. Reservations accepted. Plenty of free parking. Full bar service.

$$

Gene Sage is one restaurateur who takes his food business almost as seriously as he does his saloons. The restaurant is dark and masculine and can be noisy when crowded. While short of haute cuisine, Sage's East offers better-than-good beef and bird as well as nicely done seafoods. Let your mood be your guide as you look over the menu; there are no standouts, nor are there failures. An excellent wine list offers an extraordinarily wide range at fair prices. Desserts will make you fat and happy.

SAGE'S EAST, 181 East Lake Shore Drive, Chicago. Telephone: 944-1557. Hours: 11:30 am-1 am, Monday-Thursday; until 2 am Friday and Saturday; closed Sunday. Cards: AE, BA, CB, DC, MC and house accounts. Reservations required. Valet parking. Full bar service.

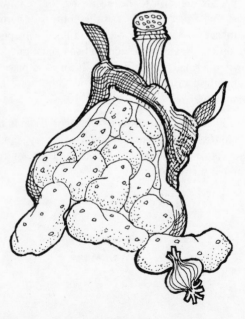

MAN'S MEAT

LE BOEUF MARLBOROUGH 7.95
CHOPPED SIRLOIN STAKE 4.95
SIRLOIN STAKE, PROFESSOR MORIARITY 7.95
VEAL IN THE MANNER OF THE
    VIRGIN QUEEN 8.50
TOURNEDOS DE BOEUF, PERIGOURDINE 8.75
RACK OF LAMB, INNS OF COURT 8.95
SIRLOIN, EARL OF SHAFTESBURY 7.95
PRIME FILET MIGNON, LORD NELSON 8.95
EYE OF THE PRIME RIB, LORD MAYOR 6.95/7.95
SIRLOIN STAKE, PRIME MINISTER 9.50
CHATEAUBRIAND, SIR ANTHONY EDEN 19.00 for 2

BIRDS & BOWLS

COQ AU VIN CHAMBERTIN 5.95
ROAST DUCKLING WILLIAM & MARY 6.95
CHYKEN, BROILED OR SAUTÉED,
    CHAMBERLAIN 4.95
CHYKEN LIVERS, ALFRED LORD TENNYSON 5.25
LE BOEUF OF THE BURGUNDIAN DUKES 6.95

FISH, MOLLUSC & CRUSTACEANS

PRAWNS DE JONGHE 6.50
CRÊPES OF ALASKAN KING CRABMEAT
    YCLEPT BILLINGSGATE 6.95
RED SNAPPER, PRINCE CONSORT 6.95
KING CRABLEGS FROM THE BERING SEA 7.95
SCAMPI FROM INDIA'S WATERS 7.95
TURBOT, CAPTURE OF CALAIS 8.95
FILET OF DOVER SOLE 7.95
LOBSTER, DUKE OF GASCONY 7.50
TWIN LOBSTER TAILS 10.00

Chicago
SALZBURGER HOF
Austrian/Continental

$$

Time was when Salzburger Hof was known strictly as an Austrian restaurant, serving delectable schnitzels, flavorful sauerbraten and fantastic nockerl. The schnitzels, sauerbraten and nockerl are still there, but recently Salzburger Hof has expanded to a continental menu. So you will find a beef Wellington, which is really boeuf en croûte with a goose liver pâté and duxelles garnish beneath the heavy pastry crust, all bathed in a red wine-based truffle sauce. You will also find other selections not usually found in Austrian or German restaurants—which only goes to show how some restaurants will change to adapt to what is commonly called "popular demand." I still favor the original Austrian delights and prefer to take my Wellington et al elsewhere. But better veal dishes, goulash or sauerbraten are hard to come by. Desserts are lusciously prepared. The nockerl and the Kaiserschmarren, a baked German pancake with apricot sauce, are house specialties.

SALZBURGER HOF RESTAURANT, 4128 North Lincoln Avenue, Chicago. Telephone: 528-6909 or 528-6855. Lunch: 11:30 am-4 pm, Monday-Saturday. Dinner: 4 pm-midnight, Monday-Saturday; noon-midnight, Sunday and holidays. Cards: AE, BA, DC, MC. Reservations accepted. Free parking in adjacent lot. Full bar service; good imported beers.

Dinners

All of Our Dinners are prepared to Your Individual Order.
Our Reputation is based on pleasing Your Tastes with Culinary Excellence.

European Specialties

Wiener Schnitzel   6.25
Thinly sliced Veal, Breaded and Sauted,
served with German Fried Potatoes
and Assorted Vegetables

Sauerbraten   5.85
The Original German Dish served with
Spatzle and Red Cabbage

Natur Schnitzel   6.95
Thinly sliced Veal, Sauted in Butter,
served with Asparagus, Carrots
and Croquette Potatoes

Smoked Thueringer   4.95
Served with Sauerkraut and
German Fried Potatoes

Hungarian Beef Goulash   5.75
Hearty Chunks of Beef, prepared in
a Piquant Paprika Sauce, served with
Spatzle and Green Beans

Kassler Rib   5.75
Smoked Pork Loin served with
Sauerkraut and German Fried Potatoes

Continental Specialties

Veal Cordon Bleu   7.25
Stuffed Breaded Veal, served with Assorted
Vegetables and German Fried Potatoes

Entrecote "Cafe de Paris"   8.75
Prime Sirloin Steak topped with melted
Herb Butter, accompanied by assorted
Vegetables and Croquette Potatoes

Escalope of Veal aux Champignons   6.95
Sliced Veal in a Fine Mushroom Sauce,
accompanied by Assorted Vegetables
and Spatzle

Venison Cutlets   9.25
Served with Vegetables Bouquetiere
and Croquette Potatoes

Steak au Poivre   8.75
Prime Sirloin Steak covered with
freshly crushed Black Pepper,
Broiled to Taste, served with
Vegetables and Croquette Potatoes

Rack of Venison for Two   24.00
Garnished with Fruit, assorted
Vegetables and Spatzle

Prime N.Y. Sirloin   8.50
Broiled to Your Taste, served with
Assorted Vegetables and Croquette Potatoes

Fish and Fowl Specialties

Frog Legs a la Maison   6.25
A generous portion of Tender Frog Legs
in a sauce of Garlic and White Wine,
served with Boiled Potatoes and Carrots

Broiled Lobster Tails   13.50
Served with Drawn Butter,
Rice, Peas and Carrots

Fresh Lake Trout or White Fish   6.25
Broiled or Poached, served with
Hollandaise Sauce, Boiled Potatoes and
Assorted Vegetables

Dover Sole, Veronique   7.95
Whole or Filet of Dover Sole, Sauted, served
in Brown Butter with Grapes or Almonds
accompanied by Boiled Potatoes and Carrots

Trout Meuniere   5.95
Boneless Fresh Water Trout sauted in
Brown Butter, served with Boiled
Potatoes and Carrots

Surf and Shore   11.50
Lobster and Filet Mignon, served with
Broiled Tomatoes and Croquette Potatoes

Roast Long Island Duckling au Mandarine   7.50
Crisp Tender Duckling in Orange Sauce,
accompanied by Rice and Red cabbage

All of the above Dinners include a variety of Soup, Fresh Bread and Butter, and a
Chef Salad with your choice of House, Thousand Island, or Garlic Dressing. (Roquefort $.50)

A La Carte

Shishkebob Flambe'   7.95
Marinated Beef Tenderloin on Skewer with Onion and Green Pepper, served with Rice,
Broiled Tomatoes, Peas and a delicate Sauce

Entrecote for Two   18.00
Prime Sirloin served with Sauce Bearnaise, Croquette Potatoes and Vegetables Bouquetiere

Chateau Briand for Two   20.00
Served with Sauce Bearnaise and Assorted Vegetables

Mixed Grill for Two   24.00
Petite Tenderloin of Beef, Veal and Pork Liver, Bacon, Chipolata, served with
Broiled Tomato, Asparagus and Croquette Potatoes

SAYAT NOVA

Armenian

$$

A decor of understated arabesque patterns and arches show-cases a small but excellently prepared menu of Armenian cuisine. Many of the main course choices can be ordered as appetizers, which gives a good opportunity to taste and sample. Better yet, order the combination platter for total variety. Among specialty items I particularly like the sarma, plump stuffings of rice and ground meat enclosed in tender grape leaves and served with a delicate lemony sauce. An interesting alternative to the conventional green salad is Sayat Nova's taboule, a mixture of cracked bulgar, parsley, mint, tomato bits and seasonings. Sayat Nova, although fairly small, is usually not so busy that you cannot linger over a couple of cups of rich Armenian coffee. The lunch-eon menu is similar to dinner; prices are considerably lower.

SAYAT NOVA, 157 East Ohio Street, Chicago. Telephone: 644-9159. Hours: 11:30 am-midnight, Monday-Saturday; 2 pm-10 pm, Sunday. Cards: BA, MC. Reservations suggested. Parking nearby. Full bar service.

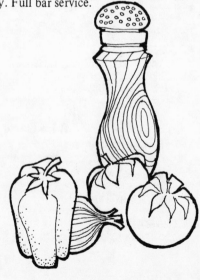

DINNERS

All dinners include soup, salad, hummos, and American coffee.
Ask your waiter for our wine and liquor selection.

1. SHISH KEBAB

Cubes of lamb meat broiled on skewers, served with rice pilaf,
broiled green peppers and tomatoes.

six dollars ninety-five cents

2. LULLA KEBAB

Ground beef and lamb meat broiled on skewers, served with
rice pilaf, broiled green peppers and tomatoes.

five dollars ninety-five cents

3. SARMA

Grape leaves stuffed with diced meat, rice and spices,
served with madzoun.

six dollars twenty-five cents

4. KUFTA

Ground meat mixed with cracked wheat, skillfully turned into balls
and stuffed with diced meat, nuts, and spices, served with madzoun.

six dollars twenty-five cents

5. COMBINATION DINNER

Sarma, kufta, eggplant and lahmejoun, served with madzoun.

six dollars fifty cents

6. LAMB CHOPS

Charcoal bromled, served with rice pilaf, broiled green peppers
and tomatoes.

seven dollars twenty-five cents

7. SAUTEED LAMB

Bite sized pieces sauteed with tomato, onion and green pepper.

six dollars fifty cents

8. STRIP STEAK

Served with rice pilaf, broiled green peppers and tomatoes.

seven dollars fifty cents

Lake Bluff
THE SILO
American

$

In classic times the students of Plato debated Truth and Beauty. In the formative years of the American republic the debate centered on government by federation or confederation. Today, we argue about the best pizza. While many Chicagoans swear by a couple of downtown spots, for my money the absolute best in the area is made and served in the far northern suburb of Lake Bluff in a restaurant that isn't even Italian. The Silo is a large, cavernous, barn-like structure with a floodlit silo adjacent to the dining area. Decor is suitably comfortable and rustic. It is exactly the kind of place you would want to take the kids or a large group of friends. The upstairs Loft is reserved for adults 23 years and older. Families and younger adults huddle at tables on the main floor. In the center of the restaurant is a large sunken bar with an open-pit fireplace. Although the menu does not appear particularly spectacular, it is studded with jewels. Start out with baskets of fried mushrooms; the mushrooms are as big as a halfback's knuckles; crisp on the outside, hot and moist within. If you like salad before your pizza you'll love The Silo salad with lots of greens, red onion and the tart house dressing. The sandwiches are large and tasty, but the pizza is the real attraction. It is thick-crust, deep-dish, almost casserole-like in its copiousness. A small 10-inch size really isn't so small at all and will feed two hungry people. The large 15-inch size takes care of a family of four with a slice or two to take home for a TV snack later. Service takes time at The Silo because everything is made from scratch, but it is time well invested.

THE SILO, 625 Rockland Road (Illinois Route 176), Lake Bluff. Telephone: 234-6660. Hours: 11:30 am-11:30 pm, Monday-Friday; 5 pm-11:30 pm, Saturday; 3:30 pm-9:30 pm, Sunday. No cards. Reservations suggested. Free parking lot. Full bar service.

Chicago
SPARTA GYROS
Greek
$

Chicago, the great hot dog city by the Lake, is being inundated by gyros. There are gyros stands springing up everywhere, a gift to us from the city's Greek restaurants. Ground beef and lamb are pressed into large rounds which are then cooked on specially designed rotisseries. But not all gyros taste alike and one of the best gyros stands is Sparta, in the heart of the New Town shopping district on the North Side. Order a gyros sandwich for $1.50 and you'll get slices of meat in a pocket of pita, the flat Levantine bread which is enjoying a new-found popularity in Chicago. Fresh slivers of raw onion, a dash of yogurt-based sauce and a couple of tomato slices are all packed into the bread pocket, making a real two-fisted sandwich. A gyros platter gives you a meal, not a snack. Other standard Greek fare such as mousaka, pastitsio and dolmades are well prepared and easy on the finances. Typically sweet Greek baklava and custards highlight the desserts. Sparta offers the hungry traveler through New Town a good haven from junk food.

SPARTA GYROS, 3205 North Broadway, Chicago. Telephone: 549-4210. Hours: 11 am-2 am, Sunday-Saturday No cards. No reservations. Street parking. Greek wines and brandy only.

Chicago
SU CASA
Mexican

$$

There are those times when Mexican food may be the order of the day, but the small and simple Latino neighborhood taco bar just won't do. When you want more than Tortilla Flats try Su Casa. Here is an antique-filled white brick-walled restaurant with the feel of a Spanish colonial hacienda in old Mexico. There are heavy wood doors, large metal ornamentation and elaborate carved statues. All dinners are prefaced with guacamole, the cooling avocado dip with bits of tomato. It is a mild contrast to the spicier fare yet to come. By the way, seasonings at Su Casa are deliberately cut back to favor American tastes—this is not authentically hot Mexican cuisine. But picante sauce at the table will bring back the hots, pronto. Among the several dinners, I always like the combination plate for an ample sample of this and that. Another favorite is the camarones a la Veracruzana. The shrimp come in the shell, heavily buttered and grilled. It is the kind of dish you can dig into with your hands.

SU CASA MEXICAN RESTAURANT, 49 East Ontario, Chicago. Telephone: 943-4041. Hours: 11:30 am-1 am, Monday-Friday; 5 pm-2 am, Saturday; closed Sunday. Cards: AE, BA, CB, DC. Reservations suggested. Valet parking. Full bar service.

SU CASA DE-LUXE COMBINATION — 7.50

A Strip of Carne Asada   ½ Chile Relleno
Cheese Taco   Chicken Enchilada
Rice   Guacamole Salad   Refried Beans
Fruit Plate or Sherbet

CARNE ASADA — 7.50

Butterfly Cut of Prime Tenderloin, Broiled
Rice   Guacamole Salad   Refried Beans
Fruit Plate or Sherbet

CAMARONES a La VERACRUZANA — 7.50

(Shrimp Veracruz Style)
Large Shrimp in the Shell, Marinated in Wine and Spices
Broiled, Served with Guacamole, Rice, Sliced Tomatoes
and Crisp Tortillas
Fruit Plate or Sherbet

TRUCHA AL CILANTRO — 5.50

(Brook Trout with fresh Coriander) Brook Trout sauted
with garlic, onion and spices. Topped with fresh coriander
and cucumber. Served with rice and fresh sliced tomato

Pollo Con Mole — 5.25 or Arroz Con Pollo — 5.25

(Chicken Mole)   (Chicken with Rice)
Served with Refried Beans and Guacamole Salad
Fruit Plate or Sherbet

friday specials

CAMARONES MARINERA — 5.50

Shrimp Sauted in a Marinera Sauce on a Bed of Rice

HUEVOS RANCHEROS — 3.75

Two Poached Eggs on a Tortilla Topped with
Ranchero Sauce

ENCHILADAS FILLED WITH CHEESE AND ONION TOPPED WITH GREEN SAUCE AND SOUR CREAM — 4.75

Served with Above Items
Guacamole Salad
Fruit Plate or Sherbet

Chicago
SWEETWATER
French

$$$

1028 North Rush, formerly the home of Mister Kelly's, is now the home of Sweetwater. At this remarkable new restaurant fine food is served in one of the most beautiful settings our city is fortunate enough to have. In the cafe, diners watch the passing parade outside, protected from the elements by glass walls. A large rectangular cocktail bar dominates the area which used to be Kelly's stage. Scores of diners can be comfortably seated in the large dining room amidst a color scheme of plum and silver. The food is French, expensive and outstanding. Among appetizer highlights is the cassolette d'escargot chablisienne. The salad Sweetwater and salad Paul Bocuse offer refreshing changes from the usual greens with tomato. Among house dinner specialties I can recommend kidneys in an excellent Dijon mustard sauce. Duck "tutti frutti" combines several different fruit flavors and textures with crispy-skinned boned duck. Much of the seafood is handled well; the bass in pastry crust is a satisfying choice. Sweetwater excels in desserts, particularly selections from the pastry cart. The wine list is moderately extensive and fairly priced.

SWEETWATER, 1028 North Rush Street, Chicago. Telephone: 944-1879. Lunch: 11:30 am-2:30 pm, daily. Dinner: 5:30 pm-11:30 pm, daily. Cards: AE, BA, MC. Reservations required. Parking in nearby garages. Full bar service.

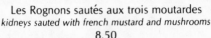

ENTREES

Les Rognons sautés aux trois moutardes
kidneys sauted with french mustard and mushrooms
8.50

Les Medaillon de veau "Piccata"
sliced loin of veal, lemon, butter
10.50

Le Poussin sauté St. Tropez
*boneless B.B. rock cornish hen sautéed with
schallots, garlic, bordaliase sauce*
9.50

La Casserolette de veau mijotée Niçoise
sautéed veal, mushrooms, peas, carrots, ripe olives, brown sauce
8.75

Les médaillons de veau "Vallée d'auge"
sliced loin of veal, pfifferlinge, mushrooms, cream, brown sauce
11.50

Le Caneton roti "Tutti Frutti"
boneless duck, bigarrade sauce, with apples, pears, orange, wild rice
9.50

Le Carré d'agneau persillé "Val Fleuri" *pour deux*
B.B. rack of lamb for two
26.00

Le Homard du maine grillé Beurre Nantais
fresh live lobster grilled with special butter sauce
14.95

Les Médaillons de Saumon poeles a l'oseille
sliced salmon with sorrel sauce
10.50

La Bouillabaisse à la mode des pêcheurs
snapper, bass, codfish, clams, mussels, ½ lb. lobster
14.95

La Darne de Red Snapper braise "Tout Paris"
champagne sauce and lobster sauce
10.50

Les Quenelles de brochet à la mode du Bugey
dumplings of pike with lobster sauce
8.50

Le Bass en croûte du chef *Specialty of S.S. France*
bass in dough with puree mushrooms in special butter sauce
10.50

Chicago
TAJ MAHAL
Indian

$$

Although not so grand as its namesake, Taj Mahal Restaurant is not without its certain charm. I like to go with a group of six or eight friends and make reservations for a small alcove in the rear of the restaurant. There, semi-secluded by a beaded curtain, diners can huddle around low tables, sit astride camel saddles or recline against a wall as the various courses are presented. Unlike some other Indian restaurants in the city, Taj Mahal serves beef dishes, but the emphasis is on the less sacred meats of lamb or chicken. Complete dinners begin with your choice of appetizer; samosa, crispy stuffed pastries, are a good start to your meal. Of the entrées, the featured specialty, tandoori murg, is recommended. A whole chicken is marinated in a seasoned red yogurt sauce and roasted in the tandoor, a special clay oven, over a bed of hot coals. Other tandoori preparations, such as lamb or boneless chicken pieces, may be among the daily non-menu specials. Curry dishes are nicely done here and are prepared to your taste, be it mild or fiery. Don't overlook the fine vegetarian entrées for which Indian cuisine is noted. Desserts are sweet, often of a cheese base and exotic in taste and texture. Barfi is much better than the name suggests; gulab jaman has a delicate flavor of rosewater. Although Taj Mahal serves wine, I suggest you drink beer or hot tea for a better flavor balance with the cuisine.

TAJ MAHAL RESTAURANT, 10 East Walton, Chicago. Telephone: 642-7446. Lunch: 11:45 am-2:30 pm, Monday-Friday. Dinner: 5:30-10:30 pm, Monday-Thursday; until 11:30 pm Friday and Saturday; 1 pm-10:30 pm, Sunday. Cards: AE, CB, DC, MC. Reservations accepted. Free parking at 25 East Walton for an hour and a half. Full bar service.

ENTREES

All of our entrees are prepared to customers' individual tastes. Please let us know your preference as to hot, medium or mild seasoning.

Taj Mahal Specialty

Tandoori Murg   5.95

whole chicken temptingly flavored with lime juice, ginger and salt, steeped for 24 hours in a yogurt marinade, coated with a blend of coriander, cumin seeds, garlic and a touch of red pepper and broiled to mouth-watering perfection. Served with Tandoori Nan (flat, oven-baked yogurt bread). 25 minutes please

Complete Dinners
($2.50 in addition to entree price.)
Includes choice of appetizer or soup plus masala dal, pickles, pappadam and beverage.

All entrees served with rice palao, puri and chutney

Gosht Kurma   5.25

cubes of tender beef cooked in a yogurt sauce containing pureed ginger root and chili peppers and flavored with coriander, cardamom seeds, cloves and garlic

Kheema Mattar   4.50

specially selected ground beef browned with onions, ginger and garlic, then cooked with tomatoes, turmeric, cumin, peppers and other spices and topped with green peas

Murg Masala   3.95

herb-marinated chicken simmered to juicy tenderness in a tomato sauce seasoned with cinnamon, garlic, ginger root, poppy seeds, cumin, peppers and other spices

Mattar Pannir (Vegetarian)   3.50

cubes of delicately seasoned cheese fried to a rich gold then simmered with ginger, garlic, coriander, tomatoes, peas, turmeric, red pepper and diced onions

Roghan Josh   5.50

lean boneless lamb seasoned with red pepper and salt, marinated in a blend of yogurt and ginger root and slowly simmered with browned onions, turmeric and coriander to a tender delight

Aloo~Gobi Sabzi (Vegetarian)   3.50

a delicious melange of cauliflower, potatoes, tomatoes and peas seasoned with coriander leaves, ginger root and other spices

Jhinga Kari   5.95

marinated fresh-water jumbo shrimp from India seasoned with ginger root, onions, turmeric, cumin, red peppers and cooked with tomatoes and coriander

Shish Kabob   5.50

juicy tender cubes of lamb marinated in a special blend of wine and herbs, skewered and broiled

Bhajia Kari (Vegetarian)   2.95

deep fried onion fritters topped with a sauce containing yogurt, mashed chick peas, garlic, ginger, mustard seed, cumin seed and exotic ground curry leaves

Chicago
TALE OF THE WHALE
Seafood

$$

Seafood and salad are the attractions here. Salmon en croûte is always topnotch and the freshwater trout tank always insures good quality for that tasty fish. A charming New England fishing village atmosphere makes you almost ready to don a sou'wester before sitting down. And then there is that salad bar, included with all dinners. To accompany crisply cold shards of lettuce there are:

Sliced peaches, sliced cucumbers, sliced green peppers,
    chopped red beets,
Cauliflower, red tomatoes, lemon wedges and
    more treats.
Lumps of blue cheese, chunks of croutons, tiny
    bacon bits
Green olives with pimiento and black olives without pits.
There's mushrooms diced and onions sliced, garbanzo
    beans called chickpeas,
Thousand Island, oil and vinegar or green goddess
    with sharp blue cheese.

TALE OF THE WHALE, 900 North Michigan, Chicago. Telephone: 944-4798. Hours: 5:30 pm-11 pm, Monday-Friday; until 11:30 Saturday; 6 pm-11 pm, Sunday. Cards: AE, BA, CB, DC, MC. Reservations required. Valet parking. Full bar service.

preface
a good place to begin

Oysters Rockefeller	2.45
Red Snapper Soup	1.50
Blue Points	1.95
Cherrystone Clams	1.95
Shrimp Cocktail	3.25
Coquille of Crabmeat	2.95
Onion Soup Gratinée	1.50
Escargots Bourguignonne	2.95
Steamed Clams	2.75

chapter I the legends

Clam Bake for Two	lobster, clams, corn on the cob, chicken, sausage	19.95
Stuffed Lobster	with mushrooms and herbs in a delicate cream sauce	11.95
Salmon En Croûte	salmon baked in pastry crust—our chef's own recipe	8.95
Maine Lobster	a whole lobster, broiled or steamed	market price

chapter II seafare

Catch of the Day	please ask your server	market price
Broiled Whitefish	lemon butter, bouquetiere of vegetables	7.95
Sea Scallops	thermidor or sautéed in butter	8.25
Filet of Boston Scrod	sautéed almondine	6.75
Filets of Boston Sole	sautéed and stuffed, topped with grapes and capers	8.50
Red Snapper	broiled, served with angel shrimp, mushrooms	8.75
Snow Crab Claws	sautéed in shallots and butter	8.50
Live Mountain Trout	fresh from the tank — sautéed	7.25
Shrimp de Jonghe	simmering in herbed butter, shallots, en casserole	9.50
Large Gulf Shrimp	sautéed in garlic butter, served on yellow rice	8.85
Seafood Brochette	scallops and king crab on yellow rice	8.75

chapter III landlubbers

Filet Mignon	9.50
Broiled Sirloin Steak	9.95

Chicago
TANGO
Continental/Seafood

$$$

Tango is an extremely modish restaurant with a cocktail lounge that looks like something out of "Clockwork Orange." The restaurant section is less harsh, although its polished tile flooring and hard plaster walls coupled with a high ceiling make the room noisier than I like. If you want more privacy, ask for seating in one of the semi-enclosed booths. Tango's sophistication encompasses an à la carte menu of finely prepared seafoods. For instance, shrimp and scallops Provençal is a fine casserole selection, perfectly seasoned with just the right touches. Fried oysters make a tasty appetizer, as does the ratatouille, either hot or cold. Bouillabaisse is as good as any I know of in Chicago. Each evening Tango also features several selections not on the menu. The variety is extensive, the fish as fresh as is possible. Service is generally pleasant and knowledgeable; waitresses are able to discuss each dish and its ingredients, should you have any questions. There are good wines on the list, reasonably priced.

TANGO, 3172 North Sheridan Road (in the Hotel Belmont), Chicago. Telephone: 935-0350. Lunch: 11 am-2 pm, Sunday-Saturday. Dinner: 5:30 pm-11:30 pm, Monday-Thursday; until 10:30 pm Sunday; until 12:30 am Friday and Saturday. Cards: AE, BA, MC. Reservations required. Valet parking ($2). Full bar service.

Entree Soup

served with warm bread, herbed butter and salad

Bouillabaisse de Marseilles   10.50
     the classic seafood dish
     of the Mediterranean

Lake Fish

served with tureen of soup, salad, rice tango and bread

Lake Superior Whitefish
     broiled   7.25
     almondine sautéed   8.25

Fresh Brook Trout, *broiled or sautéed*   8.25

Fresh Brook Trout, *stuffed with shrimp and*   9.25
     crab meat and sautéed

Broiled Walleye Pike—*when available*   7.75

Ocean Fish

served with tureen of soup, salad, rice tango and bread

Fresh Boston Scrod, *sautéed*   6.75

French Turbot
     sautéed   9.75
     almondine   10.75

Dover Sole   10.75
     sautéed and served with sauce albert

all domestic fish is flown in fresh daily;
consequently, its availability varies.

Chicago
TENKATSU
Japanese $

Except for a tearoom screen and a couple of Japanese silk prints on the walls, Tenkatsu looks like a typical American coffee shop. It is tiny, with seats for about 30 persons at a small counter, some kitchen-type tables, and booths along two side walls. The menu is printed in Japanese and English but even with transliterations you'll need some help from your waitress to understand what some of the foods are. You can be adventurous and choose octopus, eel or other unusual seafoods in one form or another. More akin to most western tastes are the tempura and beef teriyaki or sukiyaki dinner platters. Begin with suno mono, a mildly marinated sliced cucumber salad. Soup is a thin chicken broth with bits of scallion and spices. Tempura signifies deep frying; you'll get an assortment of various vegetables in a light and airy batter crust. The beef teriyaki is served as thin strips wrapped around a slice of green pepper. Sukiyaki is sautéed beef with Oriental noodles and vegetables, served steaming hot. Dinners come with lots of rice and scented pale Japanese tea. Tenkatsu is a great place to expand your knowledge and appreciation of Japanese cuisine.

TENKATSU, 3365 North Clark Street, Chicago. Telephone: 549-8697. Hours: 5 pm-10 pm, Tuesday-Friday; noon-10 pm, Saturday and Sunday. No cards. No reservations. Street parking. No alcoholic beverages.

Chicago
THAI LITTLE HOME CAFE
Thai   **$$**

Thai food is one of the best of the cuisines still largely undiscovered in the West. Yet even if you rarely stray from meat and potatoes, you may enjoy much about Thai cuisine. Although it is hot and spicy, most Thai restaurants in Chicago, including Thai Little Home Cafe, will tone down seasonings for the American palate. Count on spending about $5 to $6 per person for a full-course meal. Start with fried bean curd, a three- or four-bite cube with a crisp batter coating and creamy smooth center; dunk these pieces into a sauce of ground peanuts, oil and hot peppers. Your cheeks may flush and your eyes water, but that's part of the excitement of this exotic cuisine. The soup of shrimp and lemon grass is an excellent follow-up. The unmistakable lemony flavor is nicely balanced by other seasonings and tasty shrimp in a steaming vegetable broth. Among dinner entrée courses I heartily recommend the whole fried red snapper. The fish is tender and easy to bone right at the table. It is covered with bits of onions and small green and red hot peppers in an oil-based sauce. Easy on pepper-sensitive taste buds is a Thai-style omelette. Underneath a golden egg crown is slightly sweet ground beef in a dark sauce. Another gem is stir-fried beef and Chinese broccoli. Hot tea and soothing steamed rice round out dinners. No desserts are served, but for outstanding food in plain surroundings, Thai Little Home Cafe is a best bet and bargain buy.

THAI LITTLE HOME CAFE, 3125 West Lawrence Avenue, Chicago. Telephone: 478-3944. Hours: 11:30 am-9:30 pm, Thursday-Tuesday; closed Wednesday. Cards: BA. Reservations accepted. Street parking. No alcoholic beverages.

Chicago
THE THAI RESTAURANT
Thai

$$

The Thai Restaurant is one of the scores of ethnic finds that dot Chicago. Here you can feast like Anna and the King of Siam on marvelously exotic food. Go with another couple or two so that you can order several dishes and savor more tastes. Don't miss the spicy hot shrimp chowder. The strong bite of red chili peppers practically leaps out of the bowl, bringing tears to the eyes of even the most adventurous diner, but more subtle flavors of lemon grass and Oriental vegetables combine with the large broiled shrimp to make this soup an exquisite treat. From here you can move gingerly through the nine-page menu. Among main courses, try sliced beef in an oyster sauce that approaches liquid pearl in its smoothness. Fiery hot curried beef or palate-refreshing cold beef salad are other choices. Seafood is exceptional. Red snapper chien is the whole fish, deep fried and served under a mound of vegetables in a sweet sauce. Desserts are limited to a selection of Oriental canned fruits.

THE THAI RESTAURANT, 5143 North Clark Street, Chicago. Telephone: 334-5757. Hours: 4 pm-10 pm, Monday-Thursday; until midnight Friday and Saturday; until 10 pm Sunday. Cards: AE, BA. Reservations accepted. Street parking. No alcoholic beverages.

Special Sea Food Thai Style

Jumbo Shrimp with Garlic Cognac Sauce 4.35

กุ้งทอดกระเทียมพริกไทย.

Thai Curry Scampi with Pineapple 4.35

กุ้งผัดซอสเคอรี่กับสัปปะรส.

Jumbo Shrimp with Bean Threaded and Egg 4.19

กุ้งผัดวุ้นเส้นใส่ไข่.

Saute Shrimp with Cabbage and Mushroom 4.19

กุ้งผัด กระหล่ำปลีใส่เห็ด.

	sm.	lge.
Among The Top Treats "Pike Namdang"	5.75	6.75

ปลาไพค์ ทอดน้ำแดง.

Fried Whole Red Snapper with Sauce 5.75 6.75

ปลากะพง แดงทอดลาด ซอส.

Meat Thailand Style

Thai Curry Beef "Panangnua" 3.95

พะแนงเนื้อ

Sliced Beef with Oyster Sauce 3.95

เนื้อผัดน้ำมันหอย.

Fried Beef with Green Pepper and Tomato 3.95

เนื้อผัดพริก กับ มะเขือเทศ.

Saute Beef with Chili Pepper Sauce 3.95

เนื้อผัดพริก แบบไทย.

Beef Salad Thai Style 3.95

ยำเนื้อ

Saute Beef with Broccoli 3.95

เนื้อผัดบรอคเคอรี่.

Chicago
THAT STEAK JOYNT
Steaks

$$

This is without question my favorite steak restaurant in Chicago. It's not that the meat is better, because other steak restaurants have comparable meat. But at That Steak Joynt you can have your steak customized to an almost infinite degree. They'll grill under the gas broiler, charcoal grill, sauté, butterfly, smother in onions—you name it and That Steak Joynt will do it. This also happens to be one of the most pleasant environments around, as well as being a great restaurant. Victorian antiques and bric-a-brac, flocked red wallpaper, an ornate 19th century bar and some of the best service around make a visit here one to remember. An excellent wine list complements the meats, and there are three private-party rooms for special-occasion entertaining.

THAT STEAK JOYNT, 1610 North Wells Street, Chicago. Telephone: 943-5091. Hours: 11:30 am-2 am, Monday-Friday; 4:30 pm-3 am, Saturday; 4:30 pm-midnight, Sunday. Cards: AE, BA, CB, DC, MC. Reservations required. Two hours free parking at three nearby garages with stamped parking ticket. Full bar service.

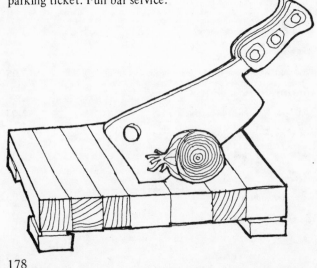

Every JOYNT STEAK is PRIME, AGED and ...

... "a cut above the usual"

Enjoy it Your Way:

char-broiled....over the open flame, until the rich natural juices threaten to burst.

sauteed victorian style.... smothered in onions and sautéed in butter sauce until it sizzles with succulence and flavor.

broiled with garlic....studded with garlic, rich and robust, for the daring gourmet.

broiled with pepper..peppercorns ground in, for those who prefer it spicy.

JOYNT SPECIALTY Rib Eye Steak, Shirlee Sauce*	7.75
PRIME BONELESS SIRLOIN STEAK New York Cut	10.50
PRIME BONELESS MINUTE SIRLOIN STEAK Smaller Edition	8.95
PRIME DOUBLE SIRLOIN For Two	21.00
PRIME FILET MIGNON Bearnaise Sauce*	9.95
PRIME BUTT STEAK Center Cut	8.25
CHATEAUBRIAND Bouquetiere For Two, Bearnaise Sauce*	21.95
FRESH GROUND SIRLOIN PLANKED STEAK Bouquetiere	5.95
TOURNEDOS OF BEEF Two Petite Filets, Saute en Butter	8.95
PIONEER BEEF TENDERLOIN Filet on a Spinach Pancake	8.25
TENDERLOIN STEAK EN BROCHETTE Rice Pilaf	7.95

ONION RINGS 1.25   MUSHROOM CAPS 2.00   BEARNAISE SAUCE .95
*upon request

other delightful delectables

PEPPER STEAK Sauteed, Green Peppers, Wine Sauce	8.95
BEEF TENDERLOIN TIPS With Chef's Wild Rice Dressing	6.95
BAR B QUE BABY BACK RIBS Special Joynt Sauce, Cole Slaw	8.50
STEAK JOYNT VICTORIA OF BEEF Pink and Tender	6.95
BROILED OR BAR B QUE CHICKEN Country Fresh	5.50
STEAK MARINER Butterflied Filet Mignon Topped with Crab Legs, Asparagus and Bearnaise Sauce	10.50
COMBINATION PETITE FILET MIGNON—LOBSTER TAIL	11.75
BROILED TWIN LOBSTER TAILS Lemon or Garlic Butter	12.75
JUMBO SHRIMP Stuffed with Crabmeat	7.50
BROILED LAKE SUPERIOR WHITEFISH Bouquetiere	7.50
WHOLE IMPORTED DOVER SOLE Amandine	9.95

included in the price of all entrees

Soup of the Day

or

Chilled Fresh Greens tossed with your favorite dressing
(Russian or Roquefort 50¢ extra)

Creamed Cole Slaw   or   Fresh Spinach Salad

and

Choice of
Baked Idaho, French Fried Potatoes, or Creamed Spinach
(Cottage Fried, Shoestring or Potato Skins 50¢ extra)

$$

Picture a typical Italian restaurant. Small Christmas lights stud plastic greenery. One wall is decorated with a mural of Venice and the Grand Canal. You'll see romantic couples alongside entire families—all seeking good food at small cost. Toscano is that kind of restaurant. It draws its regulars, but first-time customers are treated to the same cordiality and friendly service. The Tuscan sauces characteristic of northern Italy are thick and meaty, with less tomato acidity than sauces south of Rome. The menu lists the usual pastas—spaghetti, lasagna and ravioli among others. The lasagna is typically meaty; garlic is used sparingly. Among other recommended selections on the menu, Toscano chicken is mildly seasoned in a wine sauce. Veal Toscano is similarly prepared. Like many truly good restaurants, Toscano has one or two specialties which are not listed on the menu. If you like the spice of hot peppers and garlic and the richness of olive oil, ask for their special sauce. Freshly chopped parsley and anchovy add some complexity, but order this sauce on a side pasta only, unless you really like your food hot. Let your appetite and your waitress be your guide.

TOSCANO ITALIAN RESTAURANT, 2439 South Oakley Boulevard, Chicago. Telephone: 376-4841. Hours: 11 am-midnight, Tuesday-Sunday; closed Monday. No cards. Reservations suggested. Street parking. Full bar service.

Our Italian Specialties

	A la Carte	Table d'Hote
SPAGHETTI		
With Meat Sauce	$1.95	$3.15
With Meat Balls	2.65	3.85
With Mushrooms	2.85	4.05
With Chicken Livers	2.85	4.05
With Italian Sausage	2.85	4.05
Spaghetti Toscano Style Chicken Liver and Mushroom	3.75	4.95
Side Order of Spaghetti		.90
RAVIOLI		
With Meat Sauce	$2.75	$3.95
With Meat Balls	3.45	4.65
With Mushrooms	3.65	4.85
With Chicken Livers	3.65	4.85
With Italian Sausage	3.65	4.85
Ravioli Toscano Style	4.55	5.75
Side Order of Ravioli		1.10
HALF AND HALF		
With Meat Sauce	$2.75	$3.95
With Meat Balls	3.45	4.65
With Mushrooms	3.65	4.85
With Chicken Livers	3.65	4.85
With Italian Sausage	3.65	4.85
Half and Half Toscano Style	4.55	5.75
MOSTACCIOLI		
With Meat Sauce	$1.95	$3.15
With Meat Balls	2.65	3.85
With Mushrooms	2.85	4.05
With Chicken Livers	2.85	4.05
With Italian Sausage	2.85	4.05
Mostaccioli Toscano Style	3.75	4.95
Side Order		.90

CUTLETS TOSCANO

Breaded and Baked
Deliciously Tender and Juicy
Our Own Special Seasoning

$3.25 $4.45

CHICKEN TOSCANO STYLE

Disjointed, Tender and Juicy,
Cooked In Wine,
Our Own Special Seasoning

$3.25 $4.45

GNOCCHI

Homemade, Light and Fluffy,
Delightfully Prepared
In Our Own Kitchens
A Gourmet's Preference

$2.60 $3.80

LASAGNE

Baked en Casserole

Truly a Treat

$3.25 $4.45

Skokie
THE TOWER GARDEN
Continental

$$$

If awards were given for steady restaurant improvement, The Tower would win coming and going. This beautiful restaurant in a garden setting (flawed somewhat by the din of conversation reverberating against the floor-to-ceiling glass windows) has developed from a so-so suburban gathering spot into one of the best French dining rooms on the North Shore. Recommended dishes from the expensive, multipaged menu include one of the house specialties, truite au bleu, lovely trout fresh from the tank poached in court bouillon. Turbot is another treat for lovers of the briny deep's storehouse. A huge rack of lamb for two is presented to diners with a gorgeous vegetable bouquet. The tender lamb is good either with a fine bordelaise sauce or the more traditional mint jelly. Among desserts the kirschwasser torte is a taste of Bavarian charm; the crêpes à la Markus are flamed tableside and served in a coffee liqueur sauce. The Tower has without question the finest wine list in the suburbs—if not the entire metropolitan area—with emphasis on the great wines of France and Germany.

THE TOWER GARDEN AND RESTAURANT, 9925 Gross Point Road, Skokie. Telephone: OR 3-4450. Lunch: 11:30 am-3 pm, Monday-Friday. Dinner: 5 pm-10:30 pm, Monday-Friday; until 11:30 pm Saturday; 3:30 pm-9 pm, Sunday. Cards: AE, CB, DC, MC and house accounts. Reservations advised, especially weekends. Parking in adjacent lot. Full bar service.

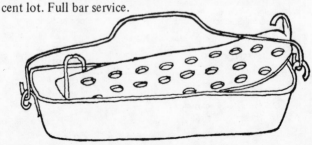

CRÊPES À LA FLORENTINE   6.95
*(Crêpes filled with Spinach Souffle
and topped with Sauce Hollandaise)*

CRÊPES À LA TOWER   8.95
*(Filled with Alaska Crabmeat in Lobster
Sauce, glazed with Sauce Hollandaise)*

SUPRÊME DE CHAPON AU CHABLIS   8.95
*(Sauteed Double Breast of Capon on
Saffron Rice with White Wine Sauce)*

SUPRÊME DE VOLAILLE "TARRAGONEZA" 9.95
*(Chicken Breast on Wild Rice,
Sauce Hollandaise with Tarragon)*

CANETON À L'ALLEMANDE   9.85
*(Long Island Duckling garnished with
Brandied Orange Slice and Grapes)*

FILET DE BOEUF À L'ITALIENNE   9.95
*(Tenderloin Tips with Green
Pepper and Wild Rice)*

FILET DE BOEUF "MARCHAND DE VIN"   10.95
*(Tenderloin Hearts on Wild Rice,
glazed with Sauce Bordelaise)*

ESCALOPES DE VEAU AU FOUR   10.95
*(Fresh Champignons, diced Veal, a la
Reine, gratinée, on Milkfed Veal)*

ESCALOPES DE VEAU A L'OSKAR   11.95
*(Asparagus Tips, King Crabmeat,
gratinée, on Milkfed Veal)*

FILET DE SANDRE "DORIA"   9.85
*(Sauteed Walleyed Pike, garnished
with Fresh Cucumbers and Capers)*

TRUITE AU BLEU   9.95
*(Freshly caught Trout poached
in a Special Court Bouillon)*

Chicago
TRUFFLES
French

$$$

Forget everything you have heard about hotel restaurants being bland. Someone in the Hyatt Regency Chicago executive suite threw away the book when they planned Truffles. This is exquisite French cuisine in a small and dimly lit dining room. While some of the luxury may be overstated, the room still projects urban dining sophistication in good taste. The restaurant's namesake, that rare Périgourdine fungus we know as a truffle, is an appetizer specialty, marinated in Cognac and champagne and baked in a light puff pastry. There are no disappointments on the menu. Sauces are perfect and dinner presentation is enhanced by the tableside preparation of fresh vegetables. Some dinner selections yield browned potatoes snuggled in a woven potato nest. This is the kind of artistry normally reserved for gourmet society dinners. Desserts are as luscious as the rest of the meal. The wine list is fairly young and, in fact, vintages are not even identified, so ask your wine steward for details.

TRUFFLES, 151 East Wacker Drive (in the Hyatt Regency Hotel), Chicago. Telephone: 565-1000. Lunch: 11:30 am-2:30 pm, Monday-Friday. Dinner: 6 pm-11 pm, Monday-Saturday. Closed Sunday. Cards: AE, CB, DC, MC. Reservations required. Parking in hotel garage. Full bar service.

Filet of Lamb a l'Ambassadrice

Prepared especially for the gourmet
with artichokes and rooster comb

14.50

Langouste a l'Emeril

Prepared in a delicate herb sauce

13.50

Dover Sole, Sautée

A whole Dover Sole, sautéed in butter

10.75

Turbot Poached or Sautéed "Naturale"

The finest of the seas, imported from France

11.00

Tournedos Beaugency

Prime center cut filet en croûton, garnished
and served with sauce Choron

12.00

Roast Duckling

Crisp Long Island duckling, served in a
delicate lingonberry
sauce, wild rice maison

9.75

Entrecôte Grillée

Prime sirloin steak, broiled to your specification,
with a delicate sauce Choron

12.25

Pheasant Souvarov

Boneless breast of pheasant in sauce
salmis, with goose liver and truffles,
wild rice maison

11.50

Médaillon of Veal

Milk-fed veal médaillons with a brandy
and chablis sauce, garnished with stuffed
artichoke bottoms

11.75

Rack of Lamb Réforme

Roasted with herbs and spices, served
with a light lamb sauce

11.25

Médaillon de Chevreuil, Chasseur

Small filets of venison saute with mushrooms,
served with wild rice maison

14.00

Veal Sweetbreads aux Morilles

Prepared with chablis and served with morels
in cream

9.75

Long Grove
VILLAGE TAVERN
American

\$\$

When was the last time a waitress stopped taking your order so she could join in singing "Happy Birthday" to a nearby table of celebrators? That's the kind of place The Village Tavern is. Located in the heart of Long Grove and its district of antique shops and boutiques, The Village Tavern crams about as much fun and food under one roof as is possible. The atmosphere is casual and boisterous. Each night brings something different—whether auction, family-style fish fry or spaghetti dinner—and on weekends there's lots of music. You cannot go home hungry. Try a 22-ounce porterhouse steak with mushrooms for $7.50, or for the same price one of the largest hunks of prime ribs of beef you've seen off the hoof. Skillet-fried chicken is $4.50 and like all dinners includes soup, salad and home-baked hot bread. Beef stew is loaded with meaty chunks and vegetables in a hearty portion for just $2.95. There's a pretty fair lineup of sandwiches and salads as well as other dinner specialties. To tell the truth, some of the food needs more seasoning, but the atmosphere and fun are zesty.

VILLAGE TAVERN, Routes 83 and 53, Long Grove. Telephone: 634-3117. Hours: 11:30 am-11 pm, Tuesday-Saturday; 1 pm-11 pm, Sunday; closed Monday. No cards. No reservations. Parking in shopping area. Full bar service.

DINNERS

Served from
5:00 P.M. Daily

All dinners are "cooked to your order" and include
tasty homemade soup, crisp garden salad with your favorite dressing
(40 cents extra if you feel like blue cheese) and hot homemade bread with butter.

Sunday at 1:00

Top Sirloin Butt Steak

A HOUSE SPECIALTY

Really Big
$5.95

Smaller
$3.95

YOU'VE NEVER
SEEN A CUT LIKE THIS—BIG OR SMALL

Prime Rib of Roast Beef au-jus

$7.50

OUR EXPERTLY PROPERLY CUT
PERFECTLY CREATED AND
SERVED AND READY TO WIN
FRAGRANCE

BARBECUED BEEF RIBS

WITH A TANGY SAUCE

$3.95

A GENEROUS RACK OF MEATY BEEF
RIBS ROASTED TO PERFECTION

22 OZ. PORTERHOUSE STEAK

SERVED WITH MUSHROOMS

THE KING OF STEAKS
TOP CHOICE, TOUCHED
WITH CHEF'S BUTTER

$7.50

2 BROILED LAMB CHOPS

DOUBLE CUT
BLUE RIBBON QUALITY

$6.75

MINT JELLY

VILLAGE STEW

A Savory Stew from
Top Sirloin Butt Trimmings
with Potatoes and Vegetables

$2.95

COUNTRY FRIED CHICKEN

PAN FRIED CAREFULLY
in an IRON SKILLET
(Allow 30 minutes)

½ ½

$4.50

SHRIMP FANTAILS

with our special Tavern Dip

6 Seasoned Jumbo Shrimps
—Crisp and Delicious

$4.50

BROILED FRESH WHITE FISH

$4.50

SERVED ONLY IN SEASON TO
INSURE ITS FRESH CAUGHT
FLAVOR

OCEAN PERCH

TWO FILETS BREADED ON THE
PREMISES AND FRIED TO A
GOLDEN BROWN — TARTAR
SAUCE

$2.95

JUMBO CHOPPED BEEFSTEAK

WITH SAUTEED ONIONS

A ROBUST HALF POUND OF TENDER,
JUICY, CHOICE MEAT INDIVIDUALLY
BROILED TO YOUR LIKING

$3.95

Chicago
THE WATERFRONT
Seafood

$$

Batten down the hatches, hoist the mainsail and steer a course for Rush Street. The decor of weathered wood, bare brick and fixtures normally seen aboard a brigantine sailing the seven seas leaves little to the imagination. You'll sit in captain's chairs or church pews at copper-topped tables. All that's missing is the gentle motion of waves and the salt smell of the sea. The Waterfront is the only place in town that I know of for cioppino. Despite its foreign-sounding name, cioppino traces its origin to San Francisco, where seamen would cook a waterfront dinner composed of delicacies from their catch. At The Waterfront, cioppino includes shrimp, oysters, clams and crab meat in a Tabasco-like hot sauce seasoned with bay leaves and spices. Served piping hot in a cast iron skillet, it is highly seasoned, not for the timid. Milder are such entrées as sole almondine, trout or red snapper. Sole en sacque, not often found on local menus, is a beautiful preparation as pleasing to the eye as it is to the palate. All dinners include access to the salad bar. In addition to the regular dinner menu, there is a lower-priced selection of snacks for lunch or weeknight after-theater crowds.

THE WATERFRONT, 1015 North Rush Street, Chicago. Telephone: 943-7494. Hours: 11:30 am-midnight, Monday-Thursday; until 1 am Friday and Saturday; 11:30 am-11 pm, Sunday. Sunday brunch: 11:30 am-3 pm. Cards: AE, BA. Reservations suggested. Parking in a city garage 1-1/2 blocks south (most reasonable rates in the entire Rush Street area). Full bar service.

Served with a selection from our gourmet
salad bar and rice pilaf

SOLE EN SACQUE
Filet of sole on a bed of thin-sliced ham stuffed
with tiny Alaskan shrimp, mushrooms and ripe olives
in our creamy sherry sauce. Baked to perfection in
parchment to preserve the natural juices and aroma
for your dining pleasure .... $ 8.50

DOVER SOLE ALMONDINE
The filet sauteed in pure creamery butter and
served with slivered almonds .... $ 8.75

BAKED RAINBOW TROUT
The whole boneless trout baked with a stuffing of
celery, ripe olives, mushrooms and herbs .... $ 8.50

PAN FRIED TROUT
The game fisherman's classic treatment .... $ 7.50

BROILED RED SNAPPER
The whole fish -- au naturale .... $ 7.75

LAKE SUPERIOR WHITEFISH
This filet of locally famous freshwater fish
is quickly broiled to perfection in lemon
butter only, to preserve its delicate flavor .... $ 7.50

MAZATLAN PRAWNS IN A PAN
Jumbo gulf shrimp sauteed in the shell in a sauce
of garlic butter, wine, mushrooms and savory
Mexican spices, served in the cooking pan. Pick
them up with your hands and sop up the wonderful
sauce with our sourdough bread .... $ 8.75

TINY BAY SCALLOPS
Sauteed in a butter and wine sauce .... $ 7.75

FROG LEGS MEUNIERE
Sauteed to perfection in savory garlic butter ...... $ 7.75

SEAFOOD MARYLAND
Lobster, shrimp, crabmeat with mushrooms in a
cream sherry sauce, baked en casserole .... $ 10.50

CIOPPINO
This San Francisco waterfront bouillabaisse is a
perfect blend of Portuguese fisherman sauce and
West Coast shellfish ... just right for dunking ..... $ 9.75

MAINE LOBSTER
Your choice steamed to order (1½ lb. av.) .... $ 13.50

LOBSTER TAILS
Two five-ounce lobster tails broiled with
lemon butter .... $ 13.75

DUNGENESS CRAB
The whole sweet San Francisco crab. Served
with lemon butter (2½ lb. av.) .... $ 9.75

Chicago
WRIGLEY BUILDING RESTAURANT
Continental

$$

Back in the time when Lisbeth Scott was making movies, when Andy Pafko was thrilling Cub fans, when chewing gum was a nickel a pack . . . back in those days Chicagoans thought of The Wrigley Building Restaurant as a place for exceptional dining. Today Scott, Pafko and nickel gum may have all changed, but The Wrigley Building Restaurant is still among the finest. Even though dwindling crowds have forced its closing on Saturday and Sunday nights, during the week it is still a stylish way to dine at moderate cost. The building itself is an architectural landmark, the largest terra cotta structure in the world, a striking white-tile, twin-peaked edifice. The restaurant represents uncompromising quality. At lunch a haven for the Boul Mich crowd, evenings will find the cavernous dining rooms less crowded and extremely comfortable. Among dinners I have enjoyed is an exceptional preparation of sweetbreads, challenging for any restaurant kitchen and particularly a surprise in one which depends so heavily on the commercial trade. Beef and other grilled meats are done with finesse. Dinners are complemented by a short but well thought out wine list.

THE WRIGLEY BUILDING RESTAURANT, 410 North Michigan Avenue, Chicago. Telephone: 944-7600. Lunch: 11:30 am-2:30 pm, Monday-Friday. Dinner: 5 pm-8:30 pm, Monday-Friday; closed Saturday and Sunday. Cards: AE, BA, CB, DC, MC. Reservations accepted. Free parking in lot behind Wrigley Building at southwest corner of Rush and Hubbard. Full bar service.

"New ideas can be good or bad, just the same as old ones."

Today's Dinner Selections

(INCLUDE OUR CHEF'S SPECIAL LIVER PATÉ, RELISHES; SOUP DU JOUR OR JUICE, SALAD, POTATO, VEGETABLE DU JOUR AND BEVERAGE)

Freshwater Fish and Seafood

WHOLE, IMPORTED, GENUINE DOVER SOLE, Saute Meuniere . . 10.50
BROILED FRESH WHITEFISH, Maitre d'Hotel (Tail Piece 75c. extra) 8.25
FRESH, GENUINE BOSTON SCHROD, GRENOBLOISE . . .
    Saute Meuniere; Lemon, Anchovy and Caper Garniture 7.25
FRESH, GENUINE CAPE COD SCALLOPS Saute aux Fines Herbes . 8.50

Entrees

BOILED, FRESH BRISKET OF BEEF; Creamy Horseradish Sauce . . 5.75
FRESH CALF'S LIVER, LYONNAISE . . . Sauteed with Onions;
    Rasher of Bacon 6.95
SUPREME OF CHICKEN, KIEV . . . Saute to Order;
    with Special Butter Filling; Demi-Glace 5.95
GENUINE VEAL SWEETBREADS, RACHEL . . . Saute au Sherry;
    Braised with Artichokes; Sauce Madere 8.25
TOURNEDOS OF PRIME BEEF TENDERLOIN, HELDER . . . Broiled
    to Order; Fotatoes Parisienne; Broiled Tomato; Sauce Bearnaise . 10.50
TWO, DOUBLE LAMB CHOPS, DUBELEY . . . Broiled;
    Garniture Fresh Mushrooms 11.25
SPECIALTY GRILLE, "MAITRE RÔTISSEUR" . . . a Delightful
    Combination of One Double French Cut Lamb Chop, Split; and
    Mignonettes of Prime Beef and Pork Tenderloin, Broiled to Order;
    Grilled Tomato, Bearnaise 12.75
BROILED NEW YORK CUT SIRLOIN STEAK; Fresh Mushroom Caps 11.25

Fresh Broccoli, Polonaise   Succotash
Potatoes, Boulangere   Baked Potato
Jordan Salad (lettuce; hearts of palm and tomato)   Combination Salad
Bleu Cheese Dressing 50c. extra

-:- OUR NEW GOURMET SPECIALTIES -:-
. . . prepared and cooked at your table by our captains

1. MAITRE MARCO'S FILET MIGNON, MAISON WRIGLEY
   . . . it's most delicious 12.95
OR:
2. FILET MIGNON AUX POIVRES VERTS DE MADAGASCAR
   . . . with Fresh Pepper corns and a delicious sauce . . . 12.95
OR:
3. THE ORIGINAL GOVIA DINA STROGONOW
   . . . a very tasty dish of slices of prime beef tenderloin
   cooked in a delicious sauce with sour cream 12.95
(Salad and Vegetable du Jour Included)

Time is an important ingredient in preparing these excellent dishes.

Chicago
ZLATA'S
Serbian

$$

The more I sample restaurants the more a common truth is driven home: The best values are found in the ethnic restaurants which dot the city. Zlata's Belgrade is a good example. The food is Serbian, prepared in the old-country way. The dishes are steeped as much in history as in sauces. Serbia has had the misfortune to be a battleground over the centuries, fought over by mighty empires. A positive aspect of this has been a cross-pollination of cultures and cuisines. Thus, you will find influences of Greek food such as musaka, an eggplant and ground beef casserole. A Turkish influence creeps in through the use of rice in some dishes. And, of course, there are the unique Balkan specialties themselves. Pjeskavica is a large chopped steak of ground beef and lamb. Cevapcici are small beef and lamb sausages. Muckalica is another grilled beef and lamb dish accented with sharper seasoning. Don't ignore such appetizers as kajmak and ajvar. Ajvar is made from fried red and green peppers, mashed and seasoned. It is not as fiery as it sounds. Kajmak is a mildly tart butter with the slight taste of cream cheese. If you really want to feel the spirit, start dinner with a glass of Slivovitz, the strong Balkan plum brandy. Don't sip it timidly, but boldy take the glass and down the liquid in one gulp. Then you are ready to feast like a Serb.

ZLATA'S BELGRADE, 1516 North Milwaukee Avenue, Chicago. Telephone: 252-9514. Hours: 5 pm-midnight, Wednesday, Thursday and Sunday; until 2 am Friday and Saturday; closed Monday and Tuesday. No cards. Reservations necessary only on weekends. Street parking can be difficult. Full bar service (wines limited to Eastern Europe).

ZLATA'S BELGRADE RESTAURANT

Kajmak	.95
Ajvar	1.25
Cheese and Meat Pita	1.25
Eggplant Musaka	4.95
Serbian Veal Goulash with	
Rice and Dumplings	4.75
Serbian Cevapčiċi	4.95
Shish-Kabob-Raznjiċi	4.95
Combination Cevapčiċi-Shish-Kabob	5.50
Serbian Muckalica	5.95
Torta/Dobosh-Chocolate	1.50
Apple Stroudle	1.25
Baklava	1.00
Shne Nokle	1.00
Coffee, Regular	.30
Coffee, Serbian	.75
Roast Veal	5.95
Chicken Paprikash	4.75
Stuffed Grape Leaves	4.25

Chicago
ZUM DEUTSCHEN ECK
German

$$

Go off the beaten path to find Zum Deutschen Eck, The German Corner. In the midst of rather ordinary-looking shops and houses, the restaurant's Old World exterior makes it a standout. Inside, a similar theme is carried out with dining at comfortable tables or booths. On weekends, at its most crowded, the restaurant is boisterous with the sounds of laughter and German music. Large steins of imported beer and a sing-along once or twice during the evening add to the fun. On week nights, Zum Deutschen Eck settles down to a quieter routine. Whenever, the food is always good. Sauerbraten, one of the specialties, is marinated for two full weeks in red wine, vinegar and spices. Then, just before the beef is about ready to get up and walk away, it is cooked in its gravies and served up hot and spicy with spaetzles, soft chewy German dumplings. Another excellent choice is braised beefsteak baked in red wine and served with cooked fresh mushrooms and fried onion slivers. It is not particularly spicy, but it has a full flavor typical of middle European cooking. Weiner schnitzel needs lots of lemon juice to add moisture lost in frying. When it is available, the veal in white wine cream sauce is excellent. Hasenpfeffer (marinated rabbit) is another seasonal favorite. Traditional German cold meat or vegetable salads set taste buds to work anticipating more good things to come. The wine list includes rarely seen German reds; one taste indicates why they are rarely seen. Stick to the whites, or better still a small mug or full liter of draft beer. Pastries are homemade. Apple strudel is semitart and flaky.

ZUM DEUTCHEN ECK, 2924 North Southport, Chicago. Telephone: 525-8121 and 525-8389. Hours: 3 pm-midnight, Monday-Thursday; until 2 am Friday; noon-3 am, Saturday; until 1 am Sunday. Cards: AE, DC. Reservations required on weekends. Street parking or in adjacent lot. Full bar service.

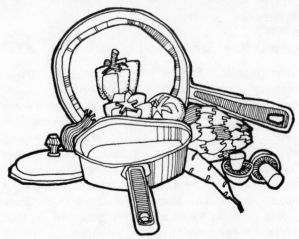

Tonight's Featured Dinners

Ochsenmaul (Meat) Salad   Chilled Tomato Juice   Homemade Suelze (Headcheese)
Chicken Liver Pate   German Celery Salad (in season)   Fresh Fruit Cocktail
German Herring Salad   Fresh Shrimp Cocktail ($1.50)

TEUFEL SALAD (Devil Salad) Julienne of Beef Tongue, Ham, Corned Beef, Pickles, Green Spanish
Olives, Green Peppers, Onions, Shallots and Mixed with a Tangy Cocktail Sauce.

or

Bavarian Lentil Soup

GERMAN SCHLACHT PLATTE	5.95
(A combination of German Delicacies including a Fresh Thueringer, a Knackwurst and a juicy tender slice of Kassler Rippchen (Smoked Pork Loin) served with sauerkraut and parsley potato)	
KASSLER RIPPCHEN	6.25
(Tender Juicy Slices of Smoked Pork Loin simmered to Perfection and served with Bavarian Red Cabbage and Parsley Potato)	
GESCHNETZELTES KALBFLEISCH, Zuericher Art mit Pilzen und Spaetzles	6.50
(Sliced Tender Veal in a White Wine Sauce with Fresh Mushrooms and Peppers)	
SCHWEINEBRATEN (Roast Loin of Pork) and Sauerkraut, Dumpling	5.75
OLD FASHION KIDNEY STEW and Parsley Potato	5.25
HASENPFEFFER (Marinated Rabbit) and Dumpling (in Season)	6.75
BEEF TENDERLOIN A LA DEUTSCH and Buttered Noodles.	6.75
(Sliced Prime Beef Tenderloin cooked in a Red Wine Sauce with Fresh Mushrooms, Green Peppers, Onions, Shallots and Tomatoes)	
BROILED FRESH FLORIDA RED SNAPPER, Maitre d'Hotel.	6.25
FRENCH FRIED JUMBO SHRIMPS and Cocktail Sauce	5.75
WIENER SCHNITZEL and Hot Potato Salad "The Pride of Vienna"	6.25
HUNGARIAN BEEF GOULASH and Buttered Noodles	5.75
SMOKED RIESEN (Giant) Thueringer Sausage and Sauerkraut.	5.50
FRESH THUERINGER SAUSAGE and Hot Potato Salad	5.25
SAUERBRATEN (Marinated Beef and Spaetzles "Germany's Most Famous Delicacy"	6.25
SCHWEINS HAXEN (Pork Shank) and Sauerkraut, Parsley Potato	5.50
BARBECUED BABY BACK RIBS and French Fried Potatoes.	7.25
(Meaty and Juicy Ribs with Just the Right Sauce)	
BEEF ROULADEN (Pig in a Blanket) and Buttered Noodles	6.50
HALF ROAST LONG ISLAND DUCKLING and Dumpling, Bavarian Red Cabbage	7.25
KING'S CUT NEW YORK STRIP SIRLOIN STEAK with French Fried Onion Rings	8.95
DER SURF UND DER TURF (A Succulent, Juicy Aged Filet and a Broiled Lobster Tail)	9.50
AGED FILET MIGNON with Mushrooms and French Fried Potatoes	8.95

Included Are:

Hot Vegetable, Cucumber Salad or Kidney Bean Salad   Assorted Rolls and Butter

Coffee, Tea or Milk

DESSERTS

Homemade Apple Strudel 75   Ice Cream or Sherbet 60
Nuss (Nut) Torte 75   Bavarian Chocolate Cream Torte 75
Bavarian Cream Cheese Cake 75   Roquefort Cheese 75

Des Plaines
ZWEIG'S
Jewish Delicatessen

$$

Located near Mill Run Theatre, this is the best Jewish delicatessen I know of in the North or Northwest suburbs. You know it's going to be good as soon as you walk in the front door and see the salamis hanging behind the carry-out counter to wrinkle and age. Zweig's menu itself appears barely different from so many other places that feature deli-style sandwiches, steaks, fried chicken and lox platters. Even the decor is like many other places, a mixture of formica and vinyl. The thing that puts Zweig's a cut above the ordinary is the honest-to-goodness quality of the food served and the enormous portions. For instance, a lox and cream cheese platter loaded with enough smoked salmon to satisfy the most dedicated loxophile comes in at $4.25, this when lox across the counter commonly sells for as much as $8 a pound in those food stores which stock it. How about a hot pastrami sandwich where layer upon layer of tangy meat is piled high on rye bread for $1.75? Most of the cold meat sandwiches are so big you almost need a "C" clamp to squeeze everything thin enough to get a bite. Four pages of menu are lodestoned with all manner of goodies, including a sensational homemade mushroom-barley soup—big, thick and chewy. If you want more than sandwiches, complete dinners in the $5 to $6 range are also offered. In short, Zweig's is a nosher's paradise.

ZWEIG'S, 8630 Golf Road, Des Plaines. Telephone: 297-4343. Hours: 5:30 am-1 am, Sunday-Thursday; until 2 am Friday and Saturday. No cards. No reservations. Free parking in lot. No alcoholic beverages.

ZWEIG'S SPECIALS

MIGHTY DOUBLE DECKER SANDWICHES
ON RYE BREAD (No Rolls), with Fresh Potato Salad,
Creamy Cole Slaw and Kosher Pickle

ZWEIG'S SPECIAL — Corned Beef, Salami,
and American Cheese **2.95**

DESPLAINES — Corned Beef, Tongue, Swiss Cheese....**2.95**

SKOKIAN — Corned Beef, Chopped Liver, Salami **2.95**

GOLFWOOD SPECIAL — Open Faced Sandwich on Rye,
served on bed of Lettuce, Sliced Turkey, Swiss Cheese,
Bacon, Tomato, Hard Boiled Egg, 1000 Island Dress. 2.95

GOURMET PLATTERS
Served with Rolls, Bagels or Bread and Butter

TWO LARGE CHUBS **3.95**
Cream Cheese, Cucumber, Sliced Tomato, Onion and Garnish

SMOKED, PEPPER or PLAIN SABLE PLATE ..**4.25**
Cream Cheese, Cucumber, Sliced Tomato, Onion and Garnish

LOX and CREAM CHEESE PLATE **4.25**
— BELLY NOVA or REGULAR —
Served with Sliced Onion, Sliced Tomato and Cucumber

JUNIOR PLATE OF THE ABOVE **3.25**

STURGEON PLATE **4.75**
Sliced Onion, Sliced Tomato, Cucumber, Cream Cheese, Musslinas

SMOKED SALMON PLATE **4.50**
Cream Cheese, Cucumber, Sliced Tomato, Onion and Garnish

JUNIOR PLATE OF STURGEON OR SALMON **3.50**

GEFILTE FISH PLATTER **2.50**
With Boiled Potato or Potato Salad, Cole Slaw

MARSHALL'S CHOPPED STEAK **3.95**
½ lb. Ground Beef Chuck mixed with Green Peppers
and Onions — — Seasoned to Taste

HERBY'S STEAK **5.20**
Skirt Tenderloin Steak cooked to please you — Smothered
with Green Peppers, Onions and Mushrooms
Choice of Potato   Cole Slaw or Salad and Dressing

Piper's Alley

Index

INDEX BY PRICE

$$$

The Bakery, 15
Chez Paul, 34-35
The Cottage, 36
Cricket's, 38-39
Doro's, 46-47
Fond de la Tour
   (Oak Brook), 58-59
Jovan, 91
La Cheminée, 98-99
La Fontaine, 102-103
La Llama, 106
Le Bastille, 110-111
Le Festival, 114-115
Le Français (Wheeling),
   116-117
Le Perroquet, 118-119
L'Escargot, 122-123
Le Titi de Paris (Palatine),
   124-125
Maxim's de Paris, 134-135
The Ninety-Fifth, 142-143
The Ritz-Carleton, 152-153
Sweetwater, 166-167
Tango, 172-173
The Tower Garden (Skokie),
   182-183
Truffles, 184-185

$$

The Abacus, 10-11
The Atlantic, 12-13
Barney's Market Club, 16-17
Bengal Lancers, 18-19
Blackhawk, 20-21
Cafe de Paris, 24-25
The Cajun House, 26-27
Casbah, 30-31
Chef Alberto's, 32-33
Dai-Ichi, 40-41
Don's Fishmarket (Skokie),
   44-45
Dragon Inn North (Glen-
   view), 48-49
Eli's The Place for Steak,
   50-51
Eugene's, 52-53
Fanny's (Evanston), 54-55
Farmer's Daughter (Orland
   Park), 56-57
Four Torches, 60-61
French Port, 62-63
Garden of Happiness, 64-65
Gaylord India Restaurant,
   66-67
Gene & Georgetti, 68-69
Giannotti's, 72-73

Grandma's Receipts, 74
Great Gritzbe's, 75
Greek Islands, 76-77
Hana East, 78-79
House of Bertini, 82-83
House of Hunan, 84-85
James Tavern (Northbrook), 88-89
Kamehachi, 92-93
Khyber, 94-95
La Bouillabaisse, 96-97
La Fontanella, 104-105
Lawrence of Oregano, 108
Lawry's, 109
Lee's Canton Cafe, 112-113
L'Épuisette, 120-121
Mategrano's, 128-129
Mathon's (Waukegan), 130-131
Miller's Pub, 136-137
Mill Race Inn (Geneva), 138
Miomir's, 139
Nantucket Cove, 140-141
Northern China, 144-145
The Palladion, 150-151
Sage's East, 156-157
Salzburger Hof, 158-159
Sayat Nova, 160-161
Su Casa, 164-165
Taj Mahal, 168-169
Tale of the Whale, 170-171
Thai Little Home Cafe, 175
The Thai Restaurant, 176-177
That Steak Joynt, 178-179
Toscano, 180-181
Village Tavern (Long Grove), 186-187
The Waterfront, 188-189

Wrigley Building Restaurant, 190-191
Zlata's, 192-193
Zum Deutschen Eck, 194-195
Zweig's (Des Plaines), 196-197

$

The Bagel, 14
The Berghoff, 22
Bon Ton Restaurant, 22-23
Bowl and Roll, 23
Captain Nemo's, 28
Chicago Pizza & Oven Grinder Company, 29
Dianna's Oppa, 42
Genessee Depot, 70
Gino's East, 71
Half Shell, 80
Hobson's Oyster Bar, 81
Hungarian Restaurant, 86
The Indian Trail (Winnetka), 87
La Choza, 100
La Poêle d'Or, 101
Les Oeufs, 126
The Magic Pan, 127
Matsuya, 132
New Japan, 146
The Original Pancake House, 147
Ostioneria Playa Azul, 149
R.J. Grunts, 154
Sauer's, 155
The Silo (Lake Bluff), 162
Sparta Gyros, 163
Tenkatsu, 174

INDEX BY CUISINE

AMERICAN/STEAKS/SANDWICHES
Barney's Market Club, 16-17
Blackhawk, 20-21
Bowl and Roll, 23
Captain Nemo's, 28
Chicago Pizza & Oven Grind Grinder Company, 29
Cricket's, 38-39
Eli's The Place for Steak, 50-51
Eugene's, 52-53
Four Torches, 60-61
Gene & Georgetti, 68-69
Genessee Depot, 70
Grandma's Receipts, 74
Great Gritzbe's, 75
House of Bertini, 82-83
The Indian Trail (Winnetka), 87
James Tavern (Northbrook), 88-89
Lawry's, 109
Miller's Pub, 136-137
Mill Race Inn (Geneva), 138
R.J. Grunts, 154
Sauer's, 155
The Silo (Lake Bluff), 162
That Steak Joynt, 178-179
Village Tavern (Long Grove), 186-187

ARMENIAN
Casbah, 30-31
Sayat Nova, 160-161

AUSTRIAN
Salzburger Hof, 158-159

BRITISH ISLES
The Atlantic, 12-13

CAJUN/CREOLE
The Cajun House, 26-27

CHINESE
The Abacus, 10-11
Dragon Inn North (Glenview), 48-49
House of Hunan, 84-85
Lee's Canton Cafe, 112-113
Northern China, 144-145

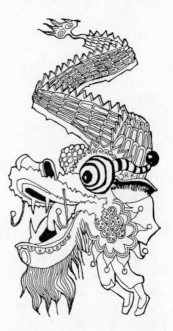

CONTINENTAL

The Bakery, 15
Chef Alberto's, 32-33
The Cottage (Calumet City), 36
Farmer's Daughter (Orland Park), 56-57
The Ritz-Carleton, 152-153
Sage's East, 156-157
Salzburger Hof, 158-159
Tango, 172-173
The Tower Garden (Skokie), 182-183
Wrigley Building Restaurant, 190-191

FRENCH

Cafe de Paris, 24-25
Chez Paul, 34-35
Cricket's 38-39
Fond de la Tour (Oak Brook), 58-59
Jovan, 91
La Bouillabaisse, 96-97
La Cheminée, 98-99
La Fontaine, 102-103
Le Bastille, 110-111
Le Festival, 114-115
Le Français (Wheeling), 116-117
Le Perroquet, 118-119
L'Épuisette, 120-121
L'Escargot, 122-123
Le Titi de Paris (Palatine), 124-125
Maxim's de Paris, 134-135
The Ninety-Fifth, 142-143
The Ritz-Carleton, 152-153
Sweetwater, 166-167
Truffles, 184-185

GERMAN

The Berghoff, 22
Sauer's, 155
Zum Deutschen Eck, 194-195

GREEK

Dianna's Oppa, 42
Greek Islands, 76-77
The Palladion, 150-151
Sparta Gyros, 163

HUNGARIAN

Bon Ton Restaurant, 22-23
Hungarian Restaurant, 86

INDIAN

Bengal Lancers, 18-19
Gaylord India Restaurant, 66-67
Khyber, 94-95
Taj Mahal, 168-169

INTERNATIONAL

Great Gritzbe's, 75

ITALIAN
Chicago Pizza & Oven
  Grinder Company, 29
Doro's, 46-47
Fanny's (Evanston), 54-55
Gene & Georgetti, 68-69
Giannotti's (Forest Park),
  72-73
Gino's East, 71
La Fontanella, 104-105
Lawrence of Oregano, 108
Mategrano's, 128-129
Toscano, 180-181

JAPANESE
Dai-Ichi, 40-41
Hana East, 78-79
Kamehachi, 92-93
Matsuya, 132
New Japan, 146
Tenkatsu, 174

JEWISH
The Bagel, 14
Zweig's, 196-197

KOREAN
Garden of Happiness, 64-65

MEXICAN
La Choza, 100
Ostioneria Playa Azul, 148
Su Casa, 164-165

OMELETTES/CRÊPES/ PANCAKES
La Poêle d'Or (Arlington
  Heights), 101
Les Oeufs, 126
The Magic Pan, 127
The Original Pancake
  House, 147

PERUVIAN
La Llama, 106

SEAFOOD
Don's Fishmarket
  (Skokie), 44-45
French Port, 62-63
Half Shell, 80
Hobson's Oyster Bar, 81
Mathon's (Waukegan)
  130-131
Nantucket Cove, 140-141
Ostioneria Playa Azul, 149
Tale of the Whale, 170-171
Tango, 172-173
The Waterfront, 188-189

SERBIAN
Miomir's, 139
Zlata's, 192-193

THAI
Thai Little Home Cafe, 175
The Thai Restaurant,
  176-177

SUNDAY BRUNCH

Cricket's, 38-39
Great Gritzbe's, 75
James Tavern (Northbrook),
  88-89
The Ninety-Fifth, 142-143
R.J. Grunts, 154
The Waterfront, 188-189

OPEN AFTER MIDNIGHT

The Atlantic, 12-13
Chef Alberto's, 32-33
Chicago Pizza and Oven
  Grinder Co., 29
Dianna's Oppa, 42
Eli's The Place for Steak,
  50-51
Eugene's, 52-53
Four Torches, 60-61
Giannotti's (Forest Park),
  72-73

Gino's East, 71
Great Gritzbe's, 75
Greek Islands, 76-77
Hana East, 78-79
Lawrence of Oregano, 108
Lee's Canton Cafe, 112-113
Maxim's de Paris, 134-135
Miller's Pub, 136-137
Miomir's, 139
Nantucket Cove, 140-141
Ostioneria Playa Azul, 149
The Palladion, 150-151
R.J. Grunts, 154
Sage's East, 156-157
Sparta Gyros, 163
Su Casa, 164-165
Tango, 172-173
That Steak Joynt, 178-179
The Waterfront, 188-189
Zum Deutschen Eck,
  194-195
Zweig's (Des Plaines),
  196-197

GEOGRAPHICAL INDEX

CHICAGO: NEAR NORTH AND NORTH SIDE

The Abacus, 10-11
The Bagel, 14
The Bakery, 15
Bengal Lancers, 18-19
Blackhawk on Pearson, 20-21
Bon Ton Restaurant, 22-23
Bowl and Roll, 23
Cafe de Paris, 24-25
The Cajun House, 26-27
Captain Nemo's, 28
Casbah, 30-31
Chef Alberto's, 32-33
Chez Paul, 34-35
Chicago Pizza & Oven Grinder Co., 29
Cricket's, 38-39
Doro's, 46-47
Eli's The Place for Steak, 50-51
Eugene's, 52-53
Four Torches, 60-61
French Port, 62-63
Garden of Happiness, 64-65
Gaylord India Restaurant, 66-67
Gene & Georgetti, 68-69
Genessee Depot, 70
Gino's East, 71
Grandma's Receipts, 74
Great Gritzbe's, 75
Half Shell, 80
Hana East, 78-79
Hobson's Oyster Bar, 81
House of Bertini, 82-83
House of Hunan, 84-85
Hungarian Restaurant, 86
Jovan, 91
Kamehachi, 92-93
Khyber, 94-95
La Bouillabaisse, 96-97
La Cheminée, 98-99
La Choza, 100
La Fontaine, 102-103
La Llama, 106
Lawrence of Oregano, 108
Lawry's, 109
Le Bastille, 110-111
Le Festival, 114-115
Le Perroquet, 118-119
L'Épuisette, 120-121
L'Escargot, 122-123
Les Oeufs, 126
The Magic Pan, 127
Matsuya, 132
Maxim's de Paris, 134-135
Miomir's, 139
Nantucket Cove, 140-141
New Japan, 146
The Ninety-Fifth, 142-143
Northern China, 144-145
The Original Pancake House, 147
The Palladion, 150-151
The Ritz-Carleton, 152-153
R.J. Grunts, 154
Sage's East, 156-157
Salzburger Hof, 158-159
Sayat Nova, 160-161
Sparta Gyros, 163
Su Casa, 164-165

Sweetwater, 166-167
Taj Mahal, 168-169
Tale of the Whale, 170-171
Tango, 172-173
Tenkatsu, 174
Thai Little Home Cafe, 175
The Thai Restaurant,
    176-177
That Steak Joynt, 178-179
The Waterfront, 188-189
Wrigley Building Restaurant,
    190-191
Zlata's, 192-193
Zum Deutschen Eck,
    194-195

CHICAGO: WEST SIDE
The Atlantic, 12-13

**CHICAGO: LOOP AND
NEAR WEST SIDE**
Barney's Market Club,
    16-17
The Berghoff, 22
Blackhawk on Wabash,
    20-21
Dai-Ichi, 40-41
Dianna's Oppa, 42
Greek Islands, 76-77
Miller's Pub, 136-137
Truffles, 184-185

**CHICAGO: SOUTH AND
SOUTHWEST SIDE**
La Fontanella, 104-105
Lee's Canton Cafe, 112-113
Mategrano's, 128-129
Ostioneria Playa Azul, 149
Sauer's, 155
Toscano, 180-181

**SUBURBS: SOUTH
AND SOUTHWEST**
The Cottage, 36
Farmer's Daughter, 56-57

**SUBURBS: NORTH
AND NORTHWEST**
Don's Fishmarket, 44-45
Dragon Inn North, 48-49
Fanny's, 54-55
The Indian Trail, 87
James Tavern, 88-89
La Poêle d'Or, 101
Le Français, 116-117
Le Titi de Paris, 124-125
Mathon's, 130-131
The Silo, 162
The Tower Garden,
    182-183
Village Tavern, 186-187
Zweig's, 196-197

SUBURBS: WEST
Fond de la Tour, 58-59
Giannotti's, 72-73
Mill Race Inn, 138

LET THESE TRUSTWORTHY GUIDES LEAD YOU TO THE BEST RESTAURANTS OF OTHER AREAS . . . .

The Best Restaurants of Texas, California and the Pacific Northwest are described in these four authoritative guides. Each is written by local food writers and critics. Each is the same size and format as *Best Restaurants of Chicago* with menus reproduced. Each is periodically revised and updated. The guides are available at bookstores in their respective areas or they may be ordered directly from the publisher for $2.95 each, plus 40 cents for postage and handling.

See Order Form on Reverse Side of This Page

ORDER FORM

Best Restaurant Guides
c/o 101 Productions
834 Mission Street
San Francisco, California 94103

Please send me your Best Restaurant guide(s) to the following area(s). Enclosed is $2.95, plus 40 cents postage and handling for each book.

_____ San Francisco and Northern California

_____ Los Angeles and Southern California

_____ Pacific Northwest _____Texas

Name _____

Address_____

City _____ State_____ Zip _____

RESTAURANT RECOMMENDATION

If you have a favorite restaurant in Chicago, not in this book, please tell us about it in the space below. Send your recommendations and comments to Best Restaurant Guides at the address above.

Name of Restaurant _____

Address _____

City _____

Type of Food _____

Your Favorite Dish _____